Hills
The Hood
Watch House
Wallsback
Watch House Creek
Rat Hill
The Marrams
Head
Channel's Mouth Sands
Cley Channel
The Cape
pe Run
ackwater Creek
New-cut
eek
Dead Mans Hole
Agar Creek
CW01669300

Once Upon a Tide

Standing stubbornly into a sea that stretches
Unbroken to the Arctic ice, it stares in the face
The winter storms that come that way ---
Salt laden-gales that drive the sea inland, scour
The beaches bend the trees and line the faces
Of its people. At times like these the north coast
Of Norfolk is a bleak and dangerous place, but
The legacy of these awesome elemental rages is a
Landscape of austere and compelling beauty
That touches all

For my dear wife
whose love and patience
underwrite all I do

First published 2014

ISBN: 978-0-9928087-6-1

Published by Whitefox Publishing Ltd. on behalf of Godfrey Sayers.

Contents

Contents

Foreword

Books about the Saltmarsh Coast of north Norfolk, once rare, are now numerous. Because they are numerous and because the top edge of East Anglia is not an undiscovered country, new titles must strive for originality. The market for books that say nothing that has not been said before is no stronger than the market for local landscapes embedded in our minds by endless and ordinary repetition. The world can manage without tepid prose, poetry and mediochre painting presented as brilliant insight.

Everyone who cares for the Saltmarsh Coast should read this book. Those who do not should read it too. You do not need to know Somerset to appreciate Cider with Rosie; you do not need to know Suffolk to be captivated by Akenfield; and you do not need to know Martha's Vineyard to be beguiled by To the Lighthouse. All you need to appreciate Once upon a Tide is a sensitivity to magic.

Incomers to north Norfolk with new eyes, fresh visions, and well-travelled imaginations have made invaluable contributions to our understanding of the place we call home. Incomers have brought energy, enterprise, acumen and ambition to its economy and enriched its culture. But an incomer could not have written this book.

It stands out from other memoirs in two ways. First, as a precious blend of local knowledge, personal experience, scientific understanding, visual thinking, wicked humour, brutal honesty, ruthless candour and environmental and social commitment. Second, it is grounded in centuries of lore and folklore handed down through forbears. As Godfrey puts it:

Generations of my family have lived here, and I am related to many of the remaining indigenous population. We are the living representatives of those who created the place, and who like ghosts in the machine remain in its charm and character. I know this place as I know my own being,

However hard incomers, including myself, try to explain why the Saltmarsh Coast is a place apart, however much we learn about its past and present, and however generously we contribute to coastal communities, we cannot become local because we were not born here. And because we were not born here we do not embody its history, culture, traditions and idiosyncrasies.

Godfrey accepts and understands that change is inevitable and that much of the change that has occurred in his lifetime has been good. But he is rightly convinced that change can and must be managed. His fingerprints and footprints are all over north Norfolk. By virtue of his friendly yet feisty personality, his willingness to go the extra mile to marshal his facts and organize his arguments and his ability to present them with a vivid combination of wit and wisdom he has won many battles between the red cliffs of Hunstanton and the white cliffs of Weybourne. He won them because he knew more than his opponents, argued his cases with greater conviction and had a clear eye for the jugular.

This book shines with examples of how Godfrey used his natural and acquired advantages to overcome his disadvantages to triumph, time after time, against the forces of (What I would call but he might not) the dark side: the side of personal and collective avarice, greed, arrogance, ignorance and self-interest. Not all possible examples appear in these pages. But enough of them are here to give the reader who does not know him a pretty good sense of the man behind the words.

Godfrey was born in a time and place where access to tertiary education - in which he would certainly have excelled - was a lottery. But had he not started life as a mussel fisherman, dug bait on frozen marshes, become a transport entrepreneur or developed the skills allied to raw talent that has made him a highly successful and sought after artist he could not have written this book. In other circumstances he might have enriched himself more but enriched the world less.

When his artistic precocity was nurtured by Bill Barnett and Alan Drury at Wells Secondary Modern School in the 1950s, Godfrey could not have imagined he would one day earn a living as an artist, have exhibitions in London and be collected by discerning collectors; that he would chair the National Trust's Advisory Body for North Norfolk, the Special Area of Conservation Advisory for the North Norfolk Coast, the Coastal Harbours Forum, Watch House Trust, his own Parish Council; and more recently the Glaven Valley Protection Group, that he would become the friend of distinguished academics and an oracle of evidence based judgement allied to common sense.

Last December, I was in London when Godfrey sent a message saying I should closely follow the weather forecasts as a tidal surge could threaten North Norfolk later in the week. On December 5 he sent another message which said the weather system was coming up five cherries. You will have to read the book to discover the meaning of his shorthand. I knew what it meant and hit the road because I trusted his judgement more than the worn out cautions of Government agencies. I returned just in time.

I trust Godfrey will live to a ripe age and will continue to dispense indispensable wisdom for many years to come. But we may not see his like again because the times and tides that made him no longer exist.

Ian Scott
Wells-next-the-Sea
August 2014

Acknowledgements

As if fired by a pinball wizard I have gone through life bumping into the most wonderful people, hitting top scores all the way. At the time it seemed like chance, but on reflection it looks a lot more as if fate may have been nudging the table. How else could I have been befriended by so many with the eyes to see something in me that I could not see for myself, and the generosity of spirit to support and encourage it.

From the very elegant lady I met as a Cub Scout, who filled in my entire Bob-A-Job card by keeping me with her for a week weeding the most enormous rose bed I had ever seen. She was the first adult friend I had, she chatted constantly and whenever I looked like flagging would say, "Don't look at all of it Godfrey, just remember, little by little and bit by bit". To Margaret Spurrell, Harry Bishop, Ronald Dew and Martin Ryle, all of whom you will meet in this book, and other more recent friends.

Ian Scott who drew me back into writing when I had more or less given it up. Mike Curtis who made me feel as if I were the most talented person he knew, all bollocks, but very encouraging. John Mitchell who did the graphics for Wiveton's Village Design Statement and in the process taught me the rudiments, and did the base grid for this book too. John Wright for verification and winnowing of the first draft. John Bond for encouragment, support and expert advice. Tim Lenton for proofreading and publishing advice. And last but by no means least Dick Girling who I met through a book project set up by Ian and who read every chapter as it was written, giving me advice and encouragement along the way and then editing it without being asked. This is their book as much as it is mine; locals and talented incomers, all have helped to shape how I feel about this short but very special stretch of coast. Yet, and perhaps this is the only reservation in this book, I should make clear that the views expressed here are entirely my own.

1 Going Native

First Visit

One of the odder predictions thrown up by quantum physics is the idea that multiple universes are constantly springing up as a consequence of chance events; the toss of a coin creating two, one for heads another for tails. My particular coin was tossed into London by Hitler - the appalling damage of the Blitz resulting in my father, who was in the police force, having a serious mental breakdown. Insignificant against the wider consequences of the Blitz but of profound importance for me. This divergence sent him into an institution and a life of solitude and introspection. It sent my mother, my baby sister and me from Kingston-upon-Thames to Norfolk; not north Norfolk, at least not to begin with, but to Burgh Castle near Yarmouth, where my mother had obtained a live-in job. Just before their marriage broke up, my mother brought me to visit my grandmother in Blakeney, the purpose of the trip I think to see if she could accommodate us in the event of a permanent separation. She was already in her eighties and had brought up fourteen children plus the illegitimate offspring of two daughters, so I can understand why she would have been reluctant, hence our first destination being Burgh Castle. All that I saw in Blakeney was so different from the urban neatness of Kingston - upon - Thames. But it was not just what I saw. Equally powerful was what I could smell. The washing strung across my grandmother's yard, the wallflowers that grew on the tops of the walls surrounding it, her outhouse leaking traces of ash and soap, and her cottage. Inside it was a rich, almost indecipherable mix of scents, a blend of substances that had had ages to soak into the fabric of that little place, few of them in general use today. Coal, candles, paraffin, fuels for softer warmer lights, lights only then going out in favour of brighter, instant electricity. During the days of my childhood I discovered that all the cottages I went into smelled the same. It was a composite smell, like flower shops and tobacconists.

My Grandmother, Mother Ginny

The most unfamiliar mix of scents was to come a little later when I wandered down to the bottom of Westgate and looked on the quay for the first time. The breath of the sea, of mud, marsh and the last Spring's tide line, and, lingering still as part of an older alchemy, tar. The ships and smacks that had been sealed with it were gone, but enough tar-encrusted detritus remained rotting into the mud of Low Quay to offer my keen four-year-old's senses the chance, just once, to touch directly a world that had gone. Like seeing that elusive green flash as the rim of the sun drops below the horizon. I am in no doubt that it was that brief touch that gave me my subsequent fascination with Blakeney's history.

I have remembered that visit often, usually when returning from extended periods away. By extended I mean months rather than weeks. It is only after those stretches of cold turkey that the smells come back with that old familiar potency, although usually only for a day or so. After that the background scents of marsh and mud recede. It was about a year after that first visit that we came up to Burgh Castle, but the work my mother was promised abruptly ceased, I suspect because of tasks not included in the job description, and we were out on the street and potentially homeless. I don't know the details but I suspect my grandmother's intransigence to our staying with her was responsible for our ending up in a small converted railway carriage near the quay at Morston. This was to be the first home in Norfolk of which I have a clear memory. The difference between it and the large three-storeyed house we had had in Kingston was bewildering. It was only the kindness of an old school friend of my mother's that gave us that small shabby roof; but for that we would have been on the street.

All my mother's aspirations had collapsed with her marriage. In a small village in north Norfolk, the idea that to improve oneself and have a decent life one had to leave was as real then as it is today. To return to no proper home or work with a small child clutching each hand must have seemed a bitter defeat. During the years before she left for London she had been fond of Billy Long, a fisherman's son. Both looking to the promises of a bigger world, they had gone their separate ways before they realised how they felt about each other. He to the Navy and eventually the war in the Mediterranean; she to a London job and then marriage. An accident with a punt gun that caused his father to lose an arm brought Billy home, returning him to the life of a fisherman. So both he and my mother were transported back to lives they'd tried to escape. During those first years I know that my mother felt very cheated and wanted only to find some way to get back to London. But as time passed her love for Billy slowly eased her regret and I know that in later life she felt it had all been for the best. She and Billy did have many happy years together. Making a good life here from scratch was not easy, however, and their happy years of retirement were very hard won.

Billy would call in on his way to or from the marsh when either wildfowling or working on the mussel lays. With my sister on one knee and me on the other, he would tell us stories woven around the life of the saltings and the sea. The characters could be ducks, seals or gulls, with names like Tom, Dick and Harry and always, somewhere thinly disguised in the plot, us. This makes them sound simplistic, but Billy was not a simple man. His 'Garnsey' and boots camouflaged one of the sharpest minds I have known. In the years ahead when I worked with him I watched many a patronising wag sail smugly up to founder on it. So those stories were well crafted, doubtless put together during the lonely hours on the mussel lays. They held us spellbound. As they grew, particularly those that became serials, I would wish the day away and, watching the door as the light faded, sit listening for his footfalls. We loved those stories and we loved him. It is of some sadness to me that he never knew how much. He was a profound influence in my later life but never more than at that time.

Who would want to live in a house when you could live in a train?

We must have come to Morston at the beginning of summer as there seemed to have been many summer days spent playing around the railway carriage and greens before I had to go to school. I had weathered the initial changes in climate well, but a brief and unexpected taste of winter came suddenly as I began my first term at Langham School.

The house we had left in Kingston was large, with several bedrooms, and bathrooms all with flushing toilets. In the railway carriage we slept all three of us in a bed that was almost as wide as the bedroom. We undressed by the flickering light of an oil lamp and went outside to a toilet of the bucket variety, installed in a small structure tacked onto the end of the carriage.

But why would you want to live in a house when you could live in a train? How many children ever got a real one to play with? My child's imagination soon had the little lavvy converted into a steam engine and the carriage into one of many stretching back toward Blakeney, the next station going east. The doors were still then original, heavy with big locks and brass handles that made that distinctive ker-lunk when slammed. I would open them all. There were actually only three (in fact when I looked recently I could find only two), which I would slam in sequence before jumping into the engine.

It was from there, bouncing on that primitive lavvy seat, that I set out on my first excursions into the lands of my imagination. So far, I have resisted the temptation to use it to explore the life I might be having in the universe where the coin came down the other way up.

2 A Country School

Lamb to the Slaughter.

On my first day at Langham School, the girl from the village who was charged with looking after me must have thought she was there to stop me falling off the bus, because the minute we got there she disappeared. Dressed in a cream and blue linen shirt with matching trousers held up by buttons attached to the shirt, white cotton socks and leather sandals, I could not have been more conspicuous if a beam of light from heaven had been shining down on me. The huge and puzzled boys that surrounded me were wearing lumberjack shirts with tank tops and long shorts of a heavy serge material that reached to their knees, where they met equally heavy-duty knitted socks coming up from large hob-nailed boots. Except when being kicked by them, these boots seemed marvellous to me. They had so many metal studs hammered into their soles that they produced showers of sparks at the slightest change of direction. Some of the more energetic boys looked as if they were rocket-powered.

My clothes set me apart, but there was more. Someone had said to my mother that I was the image of ' Bubbles', Millais' strange androgynous child in the Pears soap adverts. So before sending me out she would strive to improve the resemblance by brushing my already curly hair into an unstable and statically charged golden cloud. The only reason I survived unscathed that first day in the playground was because they didn't know what I was. I could have been a girl, but I might equally have been an elf. Once they discovered the truth, I soon acquired a closer acquaintance with the boots. I would have given anything to be like them. I didn't want to be a bully but I did want to belong, and I became convinced that having the same clothes was all it would take. I tried to persuade my mother to get me hob-nailed boots, but it was never going to work. The whole point of my clothes was to set me apart – a demonstration of my mother's belief that our having lived in Kingston-upon-Thames had transformed us into middle class.

As summer turned to autumn my hopes began to lift. Surely I would get the big trousers and boots when the cold weather came. But no, my clothing changed to a grey shirt and cardigan, grey socks and, amazingly, brogue shoes, a public schoolboy at Langham Primary. It was to be some time before I began to match the background, and even then it came through our poverty rather than any change of heart on my mother's part.

Life must have been so very hard for her then, and accepting 'hand me downs' would have been the ultimate indignity; but it's an ill wind that doesn't blow some good, and it gave me the clothes I longed for.

Finally I had the heavy trousers, the tank top and the boots, but it was still not going to work. I so wanted the horseshoe clates that made the other boys' boots spark, but I wore my heels over so badly that I had to have little half moons tacked on the edge, and they just would not spark in the same way.

Even in 1940s Langham, style was important. Snake belts had become the 'in' thing, red and white, blue and white, yellow and green, all colours in stripes. I had braces, very old braces, their weakened and wavy elastic no match for the weight of those heavy long shorts. I had begun to acquire some athleticism, certainly some fleetness of foot and a good dodging technique, but this new combination of differences put a sharp rein on that. Any rapid movement, a few happy skips even, was impossible. If I tried to leap upwards, my shorts stayed where they were, then, as the braces belatedly exerted some influence, would rush up to meet me as I came down. I had to develop the most peculiar loping gait just to be able to run and stay with my clothing. In the summer all the boys would take off their shirts at playtime to get a tan. Me, if I took off my shirt and top, it left enough room around my waist for my trousers to add spin to their separate life, and playground activities for me would have stopped altogether.

It seemed I was never going to get it right. I could try, but the pattern of difference, perhaps laid down the day my mother left for London, was ineradicable. It has been there ever since. At that time and for many years after, it seemed like a terrible and unrelenting curse but it was the best thing that ever happened to me.

As time passed things did get better and I settled in. I never felt that I was one of the boys but I was happy. It seems now like a pre-industrial world which, apart from the indirect effects of rail travel, I suppose it was. The farm in Langham still used horses on the land, and the huge big-wheeled carts were all housed in an open-faced barn directly opposite the school. At that time the rural villages of north Norfolk – i.e. those further from the towns – were virtually the same as they had been a century earlier.

The only major discord of any kind I recall after those first few weeks was the school band– not being in it but the band itself. There were about a dozen of us and, with one notable exception, no-one could play anything. The exception was George Hooke. Compared to the rest of us he was a musical genius, being able to play more than one instrument. He was a member of the Newstead family. Musicality was not common in Norfolk, so a family that could play or sing together became known for miles around. They were such a family. So on a variety of instruments that could be shaken, rattled or hit – tambourines, maracas, cymbals and triangles – we produced a mind-bending racket as we accompanied George on his flute or, on even more dreadful occasions, his trumpet. With the school on the edge of the village, I am sure the people of Langham thought themselves singularly blessed that we were not a marching band. Miss Smith, the head teacher, loved us as if we were her own. No doubt to her we sounded like the band of the Coldstream Guards, but marching and playing would have been a step too far.

She was without doubt the most gentle person I encountered in my young life. Some years later, when I had long left Langham School, I contracted osteomyelitis and spent some time in the Jenny Lind hospital in Norwich. There I received regular letters and a hamper-sized box of books, comics, sweets and Easter eggs with a card signed by all at the school. .

The other teacher at Langham School was Ellen Elwood, whom I only learned a while ago was my mother's cousin. Her resemblance to my mother in the old school photographs is so striking that I am surprised that even as a child I had not noticed it.

Recently, having at almost the last moment learned of this part of my family, I went to see her. We had a lovely afternoon and her reminiscences seemed to sharpen the focus of my own. She told me how one day a boy was quietly crying in class. She went to him, put her arm round his shoulder and asked what was wrong. " I carn't hev any mor bruthers or sisters," he sobbed. "But you already have eight brothers and a sister," she said, "and in any case how can you be so sure you won't?" "Because last night my dad went down the garden and dug up all the gooseberry bushes."

He must have been a late developer because at an earlier age than he was I knew about sex and, with varying degrees of failure, had made attempts to practise it. I met him at a party a couple of years ago with his lovely daughter, so I guess he did get through the bushes in the end.

Miss Smith

On another occasion Adrian Ropes, in whose mother's car I was later to come to school, ran in to tell her that another boy had used a bad word. "Now, now Adrian," she said, "we don't like to tell tales here. Anyway, I am sure he did no such thing." "Oh yes he did," replied Adrian. "He used the same word my father does when he's shaving."

Miss Elwood

Like Miss Smith, Ellen saw us as little angels. That particular boy was quite capable of using that sort of language. He used to collect baby birds from their nests and string them all around the gutters of farm barns. When I recounted Ellen's tale to Adrian in the pub recently he smiled ruefully and said, "Oh dear, I must have been a frightful sneak, even then."

Another little boy who was very good with his hands but had trouble with reading and writing was receiving a severe [for Ellen] reprimand. She was telling him his work was untidy and that he would have to stay behind and do it all again when Adrian interrupted her. "Miss, you said that we have to look for the good in everyone, and Freddie is very good with Plasticine." Adrian had it spot on. Freddie went on to become a master-builder cabinet-maker and a fine all-round craftsman, capable of building a house and making all the furniture to put in it. Wonderful stuff, Plasticine!

3 On the Marsh

I'm not sure how long we lived in the railway carriage, but I think it must have been about a year to eighteen months before my grandmother eventually relented and we were able to move in with her at Blakeney. My mother wanted me to continue at Langham School and her determination that I should do so, perhaps because her cousin was one of the teachers, was resolute. My having no way to get there wasn't going to put her off. The solution was that I should cycle.

My mother bought me a tricycle, brand new from a catalogue, and it was to come on the railway lorry. I couldn't believe my luck. I'd have cycled to Norwich every day for such a prize. I sat on the wall of my grandmother's yard each day for two weeks waiting for that lorry, an eternity. And then, when I had given up, it came. Throughout my life the good things have come that way, creeping up from an unexpected direction to take me by surprise. That sounds as if my wife might have leapt on me from behind, but the thrill of coming home to find the tricycle sitting there, the handlebars and seat wrapped in cardboard, stands out above any gift I have ever had.

I then cycled to Langham and back each day on it, presumably in all weathers. I don't remember any exceptions. The shortest route from Blakeney to Langham is direct, but for some reason my mother insisted that I went via Morston. The whole thing seems a bit bizarre when set against the world today, but as a child my mother walked to Langham School from Morston every day; so I expect she thought I was fortunate to have a trike. Every morning when I crested the hill down to Morston I would see how fast I could get the trike to go down the steepest bit. As I was barely seven years old and with no previous cycling experience, it was bound to end badly. In those days the road was flanked by a three-strand wire fence from the top of the hill all the way to Morston. On the last occasion that I cycled to school I overdid it, lost control, veered across the road, hit the verge and was catapulted over the fence into a cornfield. Adrian's mother came along a few moments after and saw my trike upside down on the verge with the wheels still spinning and me nowhere in sight. After retrieving me from the field she insisted that from then on I went with them in the car. A fair swap for not being able to cycle, as I'd never been in a car before. I can still remember the smell of the seats.

I continued at Langham for a couple more years and then I was moved to Blakeney School. The difference between the two was enormous. Miss Smith at Langham was gentle and kind. Miss Osborne at Blakeney was a monster. She was fat, with greasy skin, and her hands, which you had to watch all the time, had dimples where her knuckles should have been, and thick white fingers. None of these things were her fault, but sitting at her desk picking her nose was something she might have thought about, and eating it no matter how craftily she did it was not a good example for children. She had a habit of grabbing you by the skin of your neck and hitting you very hard behind the knees. I went around most of the time as if I were riding an invisible hobbyhorse. I was asked recently if she might still be alive, and while I could not guess at her age, I concluded that as she constantly recycled herself she probably is. If so, I hope she reads this. Anyway, she didn't give me much of a recommendation when I went on to Wells Secondary and I was lucky to scrape into the middle grade.

Duggy with Flo

On the very first day after the move from Morston to Blakeney, wandering up Westgate Street I met a boy of my age who had also just moved in. He approached and said his name was Douglas Harvey, and asked me if I would like to meet his mother, Flo. He took me in and introduced me to a squat little woman not much bigger than himself who had a terrible speech impediment – the result of a stroke – made worse by ill-fitting false teeth. So badly did they fit that you could hear them moving in her mouth when it was closed, particularly when she was angry. They could also stay firmly clamped together when she laughed, which she did a lot, and us laughing at her teeth made her laugh even more, and so round it went. If she had to shout loudly they could leave her mouth altogether. The word DUDDY! did it every time.

I remember her with much affection. Duggy and I became firm friends and for the next few years we were inseparable. And so my childhood began. He was the first friend I'd had, and though we grew up to lead very different lives and became very different people, there was a bond between us that lasted all our lives. We had not seen each other for several years when his wife Doreen died suddenly. I was in the USA and was distressed on ringing home to learn that the first thing he had done when it happened was to come to me and I wasn't there. He died a few years ago. Although in later life we only met a few times a year, his going has left a space I cannot easily define, almost as if he died when we were children.

Together we had adventures and a freedom quite unknown to youngsters today. We began to explore the village, becoming familiar with every passageway, loke and yard. In those days nobody questioned why you were anywhere, or what you were doing. Every big yard had a well in it. These were a fascination and we gauged the depth of each by dropping stones in. It amazed me how long it could take for them to hit the water, and the further we went up the High Street the deeper they became. Some at the highest part of the village were more than a hundred feet deep, and it seemed you could have run a hundred yards in the time it took for a stone to splash.

The very best places to explore, when we could get into them, were the old disused granaries and coal stores. Although very run down and neglected, they remained as they had been when they were in use. The old wooden steps and doors were still there, as were most of the interior fittings such as pulley wheels and wooden rollers, some almost worn through where ropes had run over them. In one granary there was an intact donkey-driven bone mill, two enormous grinding stones with a long wooden shaft onto which the donkey was harnessed. We didn't know that. We thought it was some sort of punishment device that convicted prisoners had to drag round.

What we could not have guessed was that it was the bones of dead prisoners and soldiers that had been ground up in it. The bones had come in on ships, the traffic reaching a peak during the aftermath of the Napoleonic wars, and were ground up to be spread on the land as fertilizer. For a time this part of the country was dubbed Shangri-La because the indigenous population lived so long. Apparently one prerequisite for longevity is to have plenty of selenium in your diet. Bones are rich in it, so who knows?At that time only two of the barns had been converted for other uses. One had been made into the Blakeney Hotel ballroom and the other, the long barn formerly known as Ditchell's, which adjoins a boat shed and stands with its gable end facing Low Quay, had become a dwelling.

It was playing in and around one of these barns, the one known today as North Granary, that we came upon the place that was to become our launch pad for grander exploration. My grandmother always referred to it as the Mash Green. I thought this was her Norfolk pronunciation of 'Marsh Green', but I now understand that 'Mash' may be an old English word for land with a particular proximity to the sea, particular where it provides access to a marsh path or grazing track. Along the coast many of these have stands of fennel (a plant used in cooking shellfish) just where you come off the marsh, planted long ago for those coming home with their supper.

In those days the Mash Green was a rubbish tip, a dump for the village but a treasure house for us. Among the rubbish we

found the makings of a world of our own. The area was covered with rough grass and stands of Horse Pepper (Alexanders), the hollow stems of which are tubular like bamboo. This made them usable for all sorts of things - peashooters, telescopes that made the world appear small and fuzzy, pipes for smoking old cigarette ends which made us feel sick, and the hulls of ships.

If we pulled the stalks up complete we could shape the root into a prow and the rest would remain watertight. Feathers became sails – white goose feathers were especially sought after, but if they were scarce there were plenty of others. A row of four or five stuck in along the top, a bit of broken glass pushed into the bottom for a keel, and we had as fine and functional a model ship as any boy could wish for. They only took a few minutes to make, so if one did not perform well a replacement was quickly made. By twisting the feathers to different angles they could be adjusted to sail into the wind. More ambitious models had outriggers made of smaller stalks to make them sail faster. Sometimes we would make a flotilla and set them off together at high tide, and despite having been fashioned from rubbish they made an elegant sight as they bobbed and weaved their way along the front of the quayside. Years later when I found I could sail instinctively, I realised I had done my sail training back in those days of Horse Pepper clipper ships.

It occurs to me now that the idea for those little ships had come from the older boys. I don't think we invented them for ourselves. So it seems likely that the design was being passed down from generation to generation but only through the children. So other little ships may once have bobbed along the quayside, leaning over in the same breezes that brought coal and other exotic cargoes to Blakeney in its medieval heyday. Sadly we were the last receivers of those oral packages. No other children came after us to play on the marshes. The same broom that had begun tidying up the old granaries also swept away those last small traces of Blakeney's days of sail.

Our mothers had forbidden us to go out on the marshes, but sailing those little ships took us further and further out, eventually as far as the Point, the Hood and the Watch House. On occasion we would bring back socks full of gulls' eggs, which my grandmother used to make cakes. She must have known where they came from but she always asked me to get more. Our favourite place to play was the Hood, a separate group of sand dunes lying between Cley Beach and Blakeney Point. In our imagination they could become anything – an island, a fortress, a country even, and being able to contain them in our minds made them ours. We took possession, built outposts of driftwood and fashioned big guns which we directed toward the columns of black smoke out to sea.

Over the years there have been many times when I have wanted to resurrect those forts, to set a barricade against the remorseless tide of development that has threatened this place. Long clear of ships' smoke, the northern horizon is now dominated by wind turbines, massive structures that look like a city at night and a perpetual motion machine by day. We live in a democracy but there are no guns here big enough to knock them down.

4 THE HIGH STREET

Closer to home we had a swimming hole about a quarter of a mile out from the Mash Green called Dead Man's Hole. We didn't know why it had that name but it was deep and we could dive there at low tide. 'Naked Island' nearby was our base, where we left our clothes to swim naked. The mud there was glorious. We splashed water on the banks and made mudslides, indelibly black and gooey with great smearability. We would smother ourselves with it from head to foot and run back up to the quay to perform what we imagined were African or Red Indian dances in front of the Blakeney Hotel. The guests eating their lunch must have wondered if they were not cruising on the Zambezi. On one of those days Duggy, being teased by one of the local girls, gave chase into the water and came out changed, unmistakably naked from the waist down but wearing what looked like a black pullover, his Oliver Hardy physique adding to the comedy. He then resumed the dancing, or whatever current activity the natives happened to be engaged in, oblivious to his altered appearance. The next day he told me that on his way up the High Street he had been collared by a policeman and taken home by the ear. In spite of getting a roasting from his parents as well as the policeman, he seemed not to understand what all the fuss was about, and on reflection he was right. What did a child of nine know about the problems adults have with nakedness, let alone indecent exposure?

We were on the marsh from dawn to dusk, on summer days that were a cloudless and azure blue when the water was as warm as we were full of life. We went home each day exhausted, mud in our ears, the marsh in our clothes and the scent of sea wormwood fixed in our memories for ever. All I have to do when wandering on the marsh in summer is rub some of it in my hands and, like little Horse Pepper ships, those days float back clear and untouched by the years. As long as I can find a sprig of that, the best of my childhood will always be with me.

At this time Duggy was living in the High Street (West Corner being let for the summer) just opposite what were then known as Coronation Gardens, now a car park. In those days it was an orchard, stately old apple trees amongst rough grass set out in a square with two seats on each side. In those quieter times a high value was placed on a space where one could just sit in peace. On summer evenings there would always be a couple of elderly ladies on those seats. The men preferred the seat on Quay Corner with its view over the marsh. It was the place where all the children played. There were times when the trees were as full of children as they were of fruit and, like fruit, most of them seemed to fall to the ground at some point. Out of my age group I must have been the only one to escape without a broken arm. One boy had two. On his first day out of hospital, and with his broken arm in a sling, he fell out of a tree and broke the other one. If that happened today, someone would be charged with neglect.

Duggy and his Corona Lorry

In the furthest corner of Coronation Gardens there was an almost impenetrable thicket of blackthorn and other prickly shrubs, somewhere in the midst of which an older girl and her sister gave procreation lessons. I was very keen to get in on this but I could never find them. I spent a lot of time crawling around on my hands and knees, hoping to improve my understanding of the world, but I never found them. They were in there, though, I knew they were, a belief that was spectacularly confirmed one day when a local man went beating around with a stick and half-naked children scattered in all directions.

Far more dangerous than falling out of trees were the bravery tests. By this time Duggy and I were part of a larger group which often played in and around the church. The tower door was never locked, and later when it became locked (perhaps because we had been spotted), as a choirboy I knew that the key was hidden on a hook behind my surplice in the vestry, so we were free to go up whenever we liked. In the tower's clock room there is a small door opening onto the roof of the nave. The first test was to walk out along the roof's ridge. One boy, and only one, could make it all the way to the stone cross at the far end. I never managed much more than about a third of the way – but I did remain standing.

Jacob at work

There was another test which, while less dangerous, was much more difficult and which no-one could pass. This was to climb the flagpole on the top of the tower. From the ground it looks quite small, but it is a very big pole. The problem occurred when you reached the point where the four support stays met. They were very difficult to get past, and in trying to do so you would at some point be forced to look down. When you did, oh dear, the top of the tower had shrunk to the size of a postage stamp and the illusion that if you fell you would plummet all the way to the ground was totally convincing. I'm sure most of us could have got to the top but we were beaten by that illusion.

I'm not really sure if there was more eccentricity in those days, but there was certainly a concentration in the High Street. In the yard of Duggy's temporary accommodation was old Tim Russell. Always a ladies' man, he kept chasing and dancing them at the 'Pavilion Dance Hall' in West Runton until well into his 90s. He was also very careful with his money. He had Duggy and me digging his smallholding, weeding the yard or picking his apples for a penny a day. It seemed worth it to us because we got to ride in his big old Austin 10. Immediately across the road from Tim was Jacob Holliday's shoe repair shop - not really a shop but just a small narrow room with a window onto the street. It had a row of chairs along the wall facing his worktable, and when the weather was bad the old men from Quay Corner would retreat there and fill the room with so much pipe smoke it became completely opaque. When they were not there we often were, captivated by Jacob's skilful shaping of leather and his habit of retrieving small tacks, which he held in his mouth but which appeared like magic from his long white beard.

Further up the High Street was Charlie Potterton. An exile from East London, he had a bicycle repair shop and was also the village barber. I think 'barber' might be a bit too grand for what Charlie was. He only had one style, which was a short back and sides pudding-basin cut. The first and last one he gave me had me hidden indoors for days. When asked by a customer for a DA he replied: "Only one style here, All Off!'

Everyone used Brylcreem then, or 'bwilcweem,' as he called it. Charlie's would quickly change from white to grey as he rubbed it around, fully mixing it with the bicycle oil his hands were always covered with. Charlie liked a drink and frequented the White Horse, where he would recount his battles with his wife and the other peculiar incidents that made up his life. Such as the occasion when he managed to miss the 'guzunder' pee on the electric fire in their bedroom and get flung crossways over their marriage bed. Or when his wife went to stay with her parents for the weekend and gave Charlie free rein, which resulted in him wetting the bed the night before she was due back. To try and save the situation Charlie decided to get the mattress downstairs to dry in front of the fire. On the way down it caught on a nail and disgorged a vast volume of feathers into the living room, covering the floor several inches deep. Or the occasion when she instructed him to whitewash the ceiling in the living room, and he thought he might achieve a quicker result using a stirrup pump. Richard Newton's father, who'd gone in for a haircut, said he came through looking like a ghost. Halfway through the haircut he paused, and looking thoughtfully upward said: "You know, Kenny, I'm minded to become a surgeon"

A story that gave Billy Long huge amusement was Charlie's account of a cat running blindly around his backyard with its head stuck in a salmon tin. Charlie's prequel was as follows. "We wos havin Sunday tea, an afta I put the salmon on the table I frew the tin art the winda, you know how ya do?"

Then there was Miss Jones, a straitlaced spinster who married quite late in life. Freddie (who was good with Plasticine) was working on the roof of her cottage with another builder Albert Balding. Miss Jones was telling Albert what a very nice young man she thought Fred was. "Ah well now," said Albert. "Appearances can be deceptive, you know. He's actually here on day release from prison, for work experience." "What did he do?" she asked. "He's a sex offender," Albert replied. He then left, but before going told Fred that she would be making him a cup of tea and if he went down and tapped on the window she'd bring it out to him. After a few minutes Fred did - with a startling and explosive result!

Duggy had a sister, Pauline. When I was ten she would have been sixteen, beautiful and with a model figure. Once a week she would bathe in a galvanised tin bath in front of the kitchen fire. It was a small bath. At least it was for Pauline, who so completely and wonderfully filled it. When I learned that she did this, and that the curtains – perhaps deliberately – were never quite drawn, seeing her became an irresistible fascination, and she began to fill my mind like a very bright light. I always remembered her bath day and would persuade poor Duggy that it was something we should do together. It was hard work to keep him there and usually he would go off to do other less incestuous things while I tried to make up for my missed education in Coronation Gardens.

About this time Duggy's mother had the small ice-cream shop under the clock on Blakeney Quay. Now in every way Flo was a lovely person, but not by any stretch was this true in a physical sense. Nevertheless, one afternoon at the shop, a drunk American soldier was giving her some persistent attention. I think to begin with she probably enjoyed the unaccustomed flattery, but after a while she became frightened. Each time he came back he was more drunk and more persistent. Our concern for her gave us an idea. We suggested to Flo that she invite him for tea and tell him that he could go on ahead with us while she locked up the shop. She wasn't too sure about it but was desperate enough to give it a try. He on the other hand readily agreed, and we took him off up the High Street while she went off around the quay. When we thought we had decoyed him to a safe distance, we ran off – safe, we thought, in the knowledge that his condition and lack of village geography would mean no pursuit. When we got back to Westgate Street he was nowhere to be seen.

Sometime later, when it was almost dark and we were having tea, there came a tap tap tap at the French doors. "Flo. Oh Flo!" It was him. He had found where she lived. Flo became very agitated and began having the usual problems with her teeth, uttering strings of almost incomprehensible Duddies. Duggy went very timidly to the window and, snatching the curtains back, said, "Go away, go on, clear off! ", then quickly shut them again. Undeterred, the GI began once more. " Flo, oh Flo! Please let me in."

"He isn't going to go away, is he?" said Duggy. "What are we going to do?" Our feeling that we ought to do something was given extra urgency by the realisation that what was happening was probably our fault. I suddenly thought of Pauline's bathtub, although "suddenly" might not be quite right as Pauline in her bath was never out of my mind. But it gave me an idea. "Why don't we take your tin bath upstairs, fill it with water and then tip it out of the window all over him? That ought to get rid of him!" It didn't take long to find it, and all the time we could hear the tap tap tapping and Flo Flo Floing becoming increasingly impatient. We positioned the tub on the windowsill and quickly filled it with buckets brought up from the cold tap downstairs. Soon it was full, and quietly we lifted the sash window as far as it would go. By craning out we could see the GI immediately below. He was leaning slightly forward with his hand over his eyes, peering in through the gap in the curtains that Duggy in his haste had not fully closed. This was our chance. It took both of us, but up went the bath and out went a large amount of very cold water. The result was as violent as it was unexpected. As if the icy deluge had triggered some primeval flight mechanism, he hurled himself forward with such force that he crashed right through the French doors. He was no longer outside but inside, and all hell broke loose. He was shouting, Flo was screaming, and Duggy and I were suddenly very afraid. Duggy's eyes were round. "He's gonna come up here and get us," he said, looking at the stairs. "Not down there," I said. "We'll run right into him! Down the back stairs, quick!" Three at a time we took them, through the kitchen, out the back door and we were gone, leaving poor Flo in the hands of a wet, drunk, oversexed and now enraged American madman. We ran across the field at the back and were very relieved to see that he had not given chase. Fortunately Sergeant Chapman, the village bobby, lived only a short distance away on the Langham road, so we decided to go and get him. As well as being a policeman, he was by far the biggest man in the village.

It took some time for him to take it all in. He didn't seem to believe us at first, but perhaps convinced by our fright he eventually phoned the American base.

West Corner, now Ladybird Cottage

Once they were on their way, he began to treat it as a great joke. He kept us with him for about half an hour before, with one of us in each hand, he took us back. We could see the lights long before we got into Westgate Street. What a sight met us! It was as congested with vehicles as it can get today – jeeps, trucks and vans with coloured lights flashing. We stood with Sergeant Chapman while they brought him out. I have a picture (much embroidered by time) of two very large, white-helmeted military policemen with, between them, a slumped bedraggled man who looked as he had been rescued from drowning, his hair down over his face and remnants of assorted tarts and sandwiches stuck to his ruined uniform. We spent the rest of the evening helping Flo to clean up the mess. It was a terrible mess and somewhere in the middle of it all, Flo's teeth. I didn't realise it at the time but of course it was Pauline he was after. If I'd realised then, I might have had a little more sympathy for him. From that day on, whenever I saw Sergeant Chapman he would say, "You know how to deal with the Yanks, don't ya boy!"

5 In Church

All her life my grandmother was a regular chapelgoer, and my mother too seemed to prefer chapel to church. Blakeney, she said, was High Church. I didn't know what that meant but assumed after I'd been that it was for the village worthies, the ones who looked down their noses at me. No-one who lived near us went. I had no idea why, but for some reason my mother wanted me to go to church. And so it started : Sunday School, then the choir, then becoming an acolyte and eventually carrying the cross at the head of the choir and serving as altar boy at communion. I hated it. I didn't have the God gene. The only one that showed itself there was my mischief gene. As soon as the choir had returned to the vestry I would nip out, rush to the top of the tower and pee through the gargoyles. It had a long way to fall and soon became a fine mist, but when the wind was right and not too strong I would see those old ladies, who were so good at looking down but never looked up, swatting away as if being attacked by swarms of flies. The village doctor's son would sometimes add his contribution and seemed not to notice that he was entering my class war on the wrong side. His grandfather used to bring three elderly relatives to church in his Standard 8, which he was allowed to park outside the west door.

On a day of heavy snow we rolled up the most enormous snowball, which we launched off the west side of the tower just as his grandfather was opening the doors for the ladies who were waiting to get in. The snowball impacted right in the middle of the roof. It resulted in some chaos and I guess some damage to the car, but when they looked up and saw nothing suspicious they must have assumed it just fell off the tower. Nevertheless, even as a battle in a class war it was a very irresponsible thing to do. If it had hit one of them, they'd have been dead for sure.

There were two services of Holy Communion on a Sunday, one at 7 am and the other at 11. There were two servers, the village homosexual and me - although paedophile might have been a better description. He was always after the village boys. Anyway, I detested him. He would always conspire to get the 11 am slot, so I ended up having to serve at 7 then have to go again at 11 to carry the cross. Add Evensong to that, and half my weekend was lost. The servers' duties, apart from assisting with the bread and the wine, involved striking a small standing gong at intervals during the rector's incantations. To strike it, we had what looked like a small drumstick with a felt head. On one occasion after my nine bongs I unscrewed the head to the very last thread and left it for him at the 11 am service. Having to carry the cross, I knew I would be sitting in the chancel and have a front row seat to see what happened. Sure enough, we got two bongs and a clunk. As the head came off and rolled away down the steps, he scrabbled to reach it but failed, so the rest of the chants went unaccompanied. I did it the next week and caught him again, but then thought I'd give it a rest in case he twigged. On the last of quite a number of times that it came off, it flew across the front of the altar and buried itself in a stand of dried flowers. The vicar, who had been holding the chalice aloft, put it down and turned to look at me with just the slightest grin showing. Afterwards he took me to one side and said you've had your fun, now leave him alone. I said I would as long as he'd leave me alone. He did, but I didn't.

At around that time a big passion play was staged in the church. Large curtains were hung to separate the chancel from the rest of the church and act as backstage. I was told I was in it, but being a rough council estate boy I got the small task of opening and shutting the curtains as players came on and off. I would have liked to have been tried for a bigger part. Other youngsters I'd never seen before appeared to take on some of them, but Blakeney was a different world then. The other server had a small (if over-active) part, fetching and carrying stuff on and off, so he was in and out of the curtains many times. All the players wore rope sandals, which gave me an idea. On the first night I took a packet of drawing pins and each time, just before he came through, I scattered some in front of him. He collected quite a few but there were still enough left to go round. Just about every member of the cast got a bit of discomfort, but no more than they gave me.

A new rector was appointed. On his first Sunday in the vestry during prayers, I leaned over to speak to one of the acolytes and set my Tommy Steele quiff on fire with his candle. It wasn't a major blaze, more sort of fizz and a bad smell, but it put the new incumbent against me. So a bit later when it came to Ascension Day, when the choir would process around the church, he decided to dispense with my cross-bearing services and bring back my predecessor, Curry Smith. Curry had been the village blacksmith. When I first came to Blakeney I spent many happy hours watching him at work, but by this time he had almost total amnesia. He'd forgotten where the church was, which ought to have given the new man a clue but it didn't. I watched him instructing Curry over and over, but Curry's blank expression didn't change once. Eventually, in frustration, he came to me and said, "I'm not sure that Mr Smith can remember the route, so I've told him you will give his surplice a little tug on the side he has to turn. Can you remember that?" Oh yes, I said, I could remember that.

The choir had to process slowly up the main aisle, pause briefly in front of the rood screen, turn left past the pulpit before turning back down the north aisle to return up the main aisle, where it would pause again before making a right turn to repeat the circuit down the south aisle and back up to the rood screen. Curry went off unsteadily, the cross wavering uncertainly from side to side. When we reached the rood screen he duly paused, not because he knew he should but because he didn't know what to do next. I waited a moment to make sure the rector was watching, then gave his surplice a tug on the right side. Glad to know where he was going, he set off with a surer step on his own around the south circuit. We all went the other way. He was a good way down the south aisle before he glanced across, saw us and hesitated, but it was far too late for him to turn back, so he pressed on to advance glumly towards us at the west end of the church. We had to wait a few moments for him to retake his place at our head before, proceeding again up the main aisle, he paused a second time when we got to the rood screen and to my surprise set off in the wrong direction again, and so managed two solitary circuits. The new rector may have been speaking words of love and peace but his eyes excommunicated me from them, he was furious. I might have felt there was some cruelty in what I had done, except I knew that Curry would have forgotten about it before he got back to the vestry.

This resistance to what seemed wrong or unfair must be genetic, because it started when I was still living in London and could have been no more than four years old. My mother took me to visit Santa Claus at Bentall's, where they had the most wonderful silver mock-up of an aeroplane. We went up a ramp and sat in two double rows of seats facing a screen which, once we were airborne, showed a snow-covered landscape flowing below. It vibrated and made all the right noises and was totally convincing. When we landed in Lapland we got out on the other side of the plane, sat on Santa's lap for a minute and then got turfed out into the street. I was furious. I wanted to fly back. The whole illusion was ruined, my father's Irish temper flared, and although my mother had me by one hand I began kicking out and trying to make myself too big to go through the door as I was dragged into the street. A first lesson in what life can bring.

Visiting Santa must be every child's first big disappointment. I had to be Santa once when an old boy who was supposed to be doing it was ill. I had little children on my lap asking for machine guns, motorbikes and television sets, and all I had to give them was a balloon and a heavily-wrapped packet of Smarties.

6

Three Quarter Boots

Billy's relationship with my mother would have allowed him, had he wanted, to embrace all of us as his family, but his tough character and background seemed to allow no softness toward a boy. In that fishing culture a boy would need to be hard if he were going to be any good. Powerfully built and very strong, Billy was part of a tough community. His father, 'Will Watch', was grim and weatherbeaten. With one arm[1] and pale blue powder burns splashed across his face, he was every inch a Henry Morgan. Small wonder I wanted to be on the same ship, wear thigh boots and be one of them. Much sooner than I expected I got my wish – my first lesson in be careful what you wish for. They didn't make thigh boots small enough for a nine-year-old, but they did make three-quarter boots. They didn't look quite the same but I was growing fast. I was also too young for a flat cap. I had a woollen one but I still thought I looked the part. Apart from 'Tippney' and 'Bugle' Baines, all the mussel-fishermen from Blakeney were Longs, and apart from Billy were all well over sixty – Will Watch, George, Sammy, Freddie and Fatty Long; men who had rowed the Blakeney lifeboat, fought in the First World War and grown up in a place that had hung on in an older age. A tough, hard lot that gave no quarter, not even to a child. The only time they noticed you was when you made a mistake, and then you could only tell that you had been noticed by their even more pointedly ignoring you.

George Long whimming mussels

The oldest of them, George Long, was the exception. He would always find a few words for me. George's ill-chosen nickname was 'Wongy', so for years after his death, and years after mussel-grading finished at Blakeney, the L-shaped structure he built to shelter us from storms, and which rattled in the wind, was known as 'Wongy's Latty Tat'.

The mussels were brought up from 'below' (the lower harbour) in flat-bottomed boats called canoes. Outboard motors were not used when I started, so the canoes were either rowed or punted with an oar. Rowing was easy but punting required skill. The first time I had to do it was 'down below', where the water at half tide ran like rapids over the mussel banks into the lower harbour. I was told 'go and bring that canoe down'. When I got to it there was just one oar. I succeeded in manoeuvring it through the channels but got swept a long way down the harbour at the finish. It took an age to drag it back to where they were working, where I was met with their backs and a stony silence. I eventually learned to do it and, as you will see in a later chapter, in a more dangerous situation found the use of one oar saved my life.

Mussels were brought round as seed from the Wash every three years or so in the Jane Hannah, Billy's converted Liverpool Class lifeboat, and sown in the lower harbour.

They took three to four years to mature depending on where they were sown. Summers were spent thinning them out as they grew. A hand net and rake were used to gather them on the dry; a large hooped rake with a net attached, and a twelve-foot handle called a whim, in deeper water. This was another task that had a special knack to it. It was weeks before I could bring it up with a net more than half full. A few years into the job I had one made with a couple of extra tines welded on each side of the hoop, and immediately the knack wasn't needed.

Thursday, Friday, Saturday and occasionally on a Sunday, the mussels were brought up from 'below' to the New Cut at Blakeney. We took a canoe each. Will Watch's single hand was big enough to grip and pull two oars, and sometimes when we had the tide under us I would look across to see him with the oars shipped in his lap filling his pipe. I don't recollect there being anything he couldn't do. Each canoe would be loaded as full as the weather would allow, often with just a couple of inches of freeboard. This made the return journey hazardous, the biggest danger being to hit a sandbank when running up on a big tide. The canoe could come to a dead stop and the fast-running tide would just pour in over the stern; not good in a January blizzard.

Monday, Tuesday, and Wednesday they were picked by hand – I suppose because it had always been done that way. The sheer masochism of it was never questioned. It was brutally hard on the hands, the mussels sharp with barnacles and broken shells. It took four eight-hour days to pick them. It was mind-numbing. Picking would begin by raking out a spread of mussels to the area of a small room. This had to be done vigorously and for quite a time to loosen the immensely tough threads[2] that bound them together. The mud was washed off with buckets of water – another task with a trick to it, the bucket having to be flicked in a particular way so as to get the most effective spread of water. A trick I was to employ years later making a protest in the Blakeney Hotel. It wasn't just mud that had to be washed off it was often ice and snow. We had to squat astride a basket, pick up the clumps of mussels and pull them apart with our fingers. The baskets were not strong, so some lift had to be kept in the legs so as not to squash them.

Gloves were either a hindrance or perhaps dismissed because they made the job easier. Fingernails became so worn down that at school I was accused of biting them. My fingers were hardly strong enough to pull the mussels apart at the best of times. When numb with cold it was almost impossible. In retrospect, it was as if the job was deliberately being made as hard as possible.

Billy going to the mussel beds

The first mechanical mussel-grader appeared at Morston years before anyone at Blakeney could be persuaded to even look at one. Even then they had to go through a brief period of using primitive, inefficient hand-cranked versions before getting to those with engines. At the time it seemed like Luddism but it was more likely inertia, as if the hands of all their forebears were hanging onto their jackets holding them back in the world they knew. I came to musseling – indeed to Blakeney – at the cusp of two ages. In the space of ten years it moved from the 18th to the 20th century. What I took for cruelty and hardship was just how life was. Those tough old men were so used to the levels of hardship they endured that they didn't notice. They had never known anything else.

The first purpose-designed machine we used had a single-cylinder petrol engine mounted on top. To stop it, a small metal tab had to be pressed against the spark plug to short it out. On the first day we used it, Billy put a wet finger to the tab and was hurled backwards howling in pain. That ought to have been enough to ensure that he never did it again, but it wasn't. He did it again and again. He never remembered to dry his hand, so most grading days were rounded off with a rain dance and hand-flailing howls of anguish. Waiting for it to happen, I would steel myself not to laugh. He was after all much bigger than me, and fully charged with electricity would have been far more than I could handle.

Mussel canoes

After a while he appeared to become immune, but he wasn't. He was using willpower to overcome the effects. When he put his finger on the tab a palsy would grip him, and if I listened hard I could hear a faint whimpering as his body absorbed the power the engine needed to run. It became a contest, with the engine spluttering and struggling to grab enough power to, while Billy, fully insulated in rubber boots, slowly built up enough charge to, in the words of wind farm developers, power 1,000 homes.

Perhaps those last mussel fishermen were just not suited to the modern age.[3] Over a quite short period all those old men left the cut and were not replaced. One of them sold his beds to John Wallace, who joined us on the Cut, and – when he could get there before the tide – the mussel beds.

---

1 This was the result of the accident with a punt gun that brought Billy home. Another wildfowler saw Will that day running off the marsh as fast as he could with the shattered remains of his forearm bundled up in his blood-soaked coat. If pressed, he would recount the gruesome detail of how he trimmed up the stump.

2 We sent one bag of mussels each week to a dental laboratory specifically for the study of those threads. It would have been a very pleasing symmetry if that research had developed a stronger glue for holding false teeth.

3 On the other hand Billy could be stubborn. He went and had all his teeth out and was told to return in a month to have the false ones adjusted for the shrinkage of his gums. Sadly during that month his dentist ran into the back of one of the mussel canoes and knocked the outboard off. He was spotted doing it but didn't come and own up. This infuriated Billy, as it did me, but Billy decided to boycott him and so he didn't go back for the shrinkage adjustment. This was a bad mistake. As time went by his gums shrank a lot more and the space between them and his teeth grew large. Walking beside him one day over the rough ground of Morston Strand, I could hear them rattling even when he had his mouth closed. He bought huge casks of fixing stuff but it didn't make any difference. On one occasion at sea when they became clogged with cake he coughed them out into his hand and Alan Pells, who had been at sea all his life with never so much as a hiccup, had to leave the wheelhouse and be sick.

7

John Ware Wallace

John with either Rusty or Rex

John Wallace was born in Uppingham. He was well educated and was a qualified architect and stonemason. He was also a fine historian and deserving of very much more respect than he ever got, which is why he is included here. What defined him during his life in Blakeney were his fits. I kept company with him for many years and knew him to be a gentle and compassionate if impractical man, whose intelligence and kind nature were totally obscured because of them. Wanting desperately to be a part of the village he loved, he couldn't have had a worse affliction. Simple epilepsy would have been difficult, but what John had was much worse. His attacks were brought on by stress, mental or physical, and in

their grip his emotional turmoil played him like a marionette, his innermost thoughts acted out. It was like Tourette's in mime, a horrible affliction that troubled him deeply. How many of us would want such a window into our soul?

I witnessed a great many of his fits in all their forms, and always he would ask afterwards what had happened. He knew from people's reactions that he had done odd things, but nobody ever told him, and neither did I. I say nobody ever told him but the two old ladies he took out for a row in one of his small dinghies and then exposed himself to might have said something, though I never knew whether or not they leapt out and swam to shore.

I learned as a governor of a special school that there is humour in the strangest places, and John had fits in the strangest places. He served on Blakeney Parish Council, and at their AGM, the councillors would sit on the stage of the British Legion Hall, this was always difficult for him. On one occasion when it all got very heated, he suddenly leapt up, went to the front of the stage, took his trousers down and, swinging round (no pants), 'mooned' the parishioners. How I would love to have done that. One of the councillors, was given the task of taking him home. After accompanying him the short distance to his cottage and bundling him through his front door, he managed to find time for a quick

pint before going back into the meeting. When he did, John was already back in his seat, confused but otherwise perfectly fine and quite unaware that anything was amiss. Another time, a tenant of John's invited him for Sunday lunch with his family. John had a fit, took off all his clothes, got up onto the table and performed a dance. He was quite a big man but he managed to move gracefully among the condiments and cutlery without dislodging a piece.

It was probably his parents' embarrassment of having him around in Uppingham that had resulted in his exile to Blakeney. But he made a life for himself down on the Carnser, renting out small rowing tubs to visitors, who he always referred to as 'Leicester Devils' and harassed them for sitting on boats or throwing stones in the quay. He was so pleased to finally get a mussel bed and a grading spot on the Cut. It really made him feel a part of things. Of the extent to which he wasn't, he was blissfully unaware. It was of some credit to those last old fishermen that this was so. He never knew the lengths they went to, to keep him safe. John didn't sell many mussels and his customers always complained that his sacks contained too much 'beach'. There cannot have been anyone more unsuited to being a mussel fisherman, but like so many in such situations he was sublimely happy in his illusory world.

When the first hand-operated mussel grading machines appeared on the Cut he had to have one, even though his tiny output hardly merited it. The machine he finally had made defied all mechanical laws and turned the basic mechanics of mussel-graders upside down. These early machines used a very simple principle of a turned handle and a reduction gear that converted each revolution of the handle into four back-and-forth movements of a sorting tray. John's worked in reverse, the handle having to be turned four times to get the tray to move back once. He wasn't a fast mover but the speed at which he turned that handle was incredible. His arm would become a blur and the whole process would turn into a frenzy. After a period of frantic handle-turning he would grab a bucket, rush down to the channel, fill it with water, rush back up and throw it on the sorting tray.

Blakeney from the Mussel Grounds

On one occasion two mystified visitors who were watching and standing much too close got a whole bucketful in their faces. Inevitably the stress of all this exertion brought on more of his fits, so we would often look up to see him writhing on the ground, standing to attention or taking his clothes off.

Working on the New Cut sorting mussels was – fits apart – relatively safe for him, if not for others. But of course, like us, he had to take his canoe 'down below' to the mussel lays to get them. Being devoid of any useful boat-handling skills, he was always late getting there. Sometimes he never arrived at all. I remember one morning Billy and I were working together to fill one canoe when John appeared, hopelessly late as usual. Seeing him rowing toward us, and anticipating his first question, Billy asked me the time. It was five past twelve. Reaching us, John said, "Have you got the time, Billy"? Billy then shaded his eyes and stared off toward Blakeney church tower, tiny on the far horizon and barely visible through the haze. "The church clock says five past twelve, John." John's mouth dropped open in amazement, and he kept looking back and forth from Billy to the distant church, speechless. He then pushed off and punted clumsily away in small circles down to where 'Fatty' Long was working. He stopped and began talking, and we saw 'Fatty' pull out his watch and tell John the time.

John looked back toward us, pointing and brushing his forehead in disbelief. From that day on, he would never miss an opportunity to tell people that Billy Long had better eyesight than anyone he had ever met. Billy could certainly see into John's literal mind.

Coming back from the lays was always difficult because we had to go ahead so that John could follow the channel. This almost invariably meant that when we took the ground with our fully loaded canoes, his with its lighter load, the tide under it and under minimal control, would come careering along and crash into us. This would always make Billy furious but, because it was so certain and John never ever saw it coming, it always made me laugh.

Later when I had a haulage business I would take John to the station whenever he was going away. On one occasion he was travelling to Scotland to stay with his cousin, who he said was always leaping on him and trying to get him into bed. He hated that and thought she was mad – she probably was – but he still went. I collected him from 96 High Street in a half-ton van with sliding doors. He came out laden with a suitcase, two large canvas kitbags and Rusty[1] on a lead. He approached from round the back of the van so I didn't see him get hold of the door handle. I became aware that he had because the van suddenly began rocking violently from side to side. Having assumed that the door opened outwards, he had begun pulling it with all his might. It was only after some minutes of my shouting that he stopped and I was able to slide it open for him. The trip to Norwich was uneventful. This was unusual, as most of my trips with him would involve a fit somewhere en route; rain on the windscreen guaranteed them. Not funny in a moving vehicle. On one occasion he got down on the floor and got hold of my feet. I had to make deliveries to Norwich Fish Market, and not wanting to negotiate the station car park I told John I would drop him at the bottom of Prince of Wales Road. Choosing an empty stretch of pavement, I stopped. Eager to get out, and again failing to understand how the doors worked, he threw all his weight against the passenger door, thereby lifting it off its track and causing it to burst outward onto the pavement. He went with it, landing on his back. He lay spreadeagled on top of it with his baggage on top of him, and poor old Rusty, who also got

John's Causeway

John spent several decades of his life rebuilding by hand the old Carnser that led from the sheep bridge down to the New Cut. This was of great benefit to the mussel fishermen but I don't think one of them ever thanked him. It is known now as John's Causway and belatedly the village did put a plaque there to commemorate his work.

whipped out by his lead, on top of that. John was completely helpless. The door was curved and he looked like an enormous tortoise as he rocked gently back and forth, kicking his legs and waving his arms. Passers-by were giving him a wide berth, and I was so angry I almost left him there. I had to drive home on a cold winter's day with the passenger door in the back. John was to become part of the reason I joined Blakeney Parish Council. He erected three small benches on the Carnser. Made from driftwood, they fitted in perfectly and offered a seat and a view to weary walkers. But because he hadn't asked their permission (which he didn't need anyway) the council stepped in and removed them. Equally quickly, a small group of us put them back with a warning to the council that each time they removed them we would replace them. All the years he lived in Blakeney, John's parents had sent him an allowance. He lived frugally and as the money mounted up he would buy a cottage and put a village family in it. For a short while we lived in one. When his parents died he came into more money, and bought more, all of which were rented to locals. When he died he left 12 cottages to the Blakeney Housing Society, worth about £3.5 million at today's values. Nobody ever gave Blakeney so much and got so little in return.

---

1. To a greater or lesser degree, all the dogs John had (all called either Rusty or Rex) could tell when one of his fits was approaching and would try to warn him. The largest of these, and the one that came in the van with us, would jump up and hang by its teeth on the front of his pullover. On one occasion as John wandered through the fit his pullover slowly unravelled until Rusty was wrapped in wool and all John had was a woolly ruff. What visitors who got caught up in them thought, I cannot imagine.

8 The 1953 Storm

Sudden momentous events can have an almost atomic flash effect, imprinting indelibly on our minds the coincidental events in our own lives. No detail seems too small to register, and although it is sixty years since that particular bomb went off I can remember the two days of the '53 floods in Blakeney more clearly than yesterday. We were crusaders and there were five of us. Equipped with home-made wooden swords and dustbin-lid shields, we were a small but formidable force. After some sustained heavy fighting, much of it among ourselves, we cornered the enemy in one of the yards near the top of the High Street. The fighting continued, and eventually the yard became so clogged with enemy dead that we were forced into an adjoining garden belonging to the family of one of the boys. Pausing for breath, someone suggested we look in his shed to see if we could find anything else to supplement our gear. After rummaging around for a while we found a box of gas masks. There were five of them. Just right, perhaps, but not exactly right, as there were four of the conventional type and another very odd one. Here the very slight inequality of being a latecomer – ie not actually born here – came into play, so I got that one. This small distinctive 'birth-mark' has stayed with me throughout my life. Only now, as I get older is it beginning to fade. Their masks had a single faceplate like a diver's mask, and a filter device that stuck out in front like a pig's snout with many tiny holes in the end. Mine had two flat glass eye-holes and sprouted a hideous and indecent proboscis from a plate covering the mouth, a ribbed rubber tube about two feet long on the end of which was a canister. In action it swung about so much that good swordsmanship became difficult. A few years later in Holt cinema I saw myself as I looked that day emerging from a matter transference device in The Fly.

Gathering our weapons, and now fully equipped to fight in the wrong war, we set off in search of the enemy. We hadn't far to go. As we entered the street a second wave of the enemy chose that moment to attack, and although we were vastly outnumbered the ferocity of our response was such that they quickly fell back and we had to give chase. The chase became a rout. Whooping and waving our swords, we pursued them down the length of the High Street. Reaching the bottom where the buildings open out, we met the wind. It slowed our running, first to a walk, then to a stagger, and eventually to just weaving from one side of the street to the other, holding onto the walls. The Infidel, being less substantial, made good their escape around Quay Corner. We struggled up onto Mariners Hill, which overlooks the marsh. When we took off our gas masks the force of the wind in our eyes was so painful that we had to either close them or turn away. Without our masks we couldn't face it. I remember thinking it very strange that on the same day as we were wearing gas masks we had found a place where it was impossible to see or breathe without them. One of us, struggling forward to the lip of the hill, in a brief respite launched his dustbin lid, frisbee-style, out into the wind. Lifting toward the north-east, it hung just momentarily at the end of its trajectory, then as if no more than a leaf the next gust snatched it away. Over the rooftops, over the trees and away, rising rather than falling, disappearing only when it became too small to see. Crouching on hands and knees, clutching handfuls of grass to avoid being blown over, it was clear to us that we were in the middle of something extraordinary.

One of the boys lived near me in Westgate Street and we would usually walk home together along the quayside. Aiming to do that, we made our way down the hill toward the quay, and by keeping close to the old coal barns on the west side of the street we were able to cheat the wind. It was at Quay Corner that we met its full fury. In the years since then I have seen my share of bad weather, particularly during my time in the Navy and occasionally on smaller boats. But never have I experienced a wind like that. It was not possible to make any progress against it. Determined to try, we crawled across the road on our hands and knees. Reaching the wooden railings that went round the quayside, we pulled ourselves to our feet and then, hanging on like wing-walkers, faces distorted and hair swept back, held on for dear life. Clearly we could not go home the way we intended. Even retracing our steps would see us blown flat on our faces. So, slowly, we lowered ourselves down on all fours and retreated the way we had come, then made our way back up the High Street and home through a sheltered lane.

The evening of that day found my mother and I taking coal up to our recently allocated and newly-built council house. We had been keeping fires going to air it out. Leaving my grandmother's yard we could see that the tide was into the bottom of Westgate Street. We were away little more than 20 minutes, but when we got back the tide was running into our own yard halfway up the street. Remarkably, the power was still on and by the lights of the King's Arms I could see a man rowing a mussel canoe up the street. It was Billy 'Bugle' Baines. He told me much later that the canoe needed tarring, so he thought he would take the opportunity to take it home the easy way. If that were true (he may well have had more pressing reasons that night than general maintenance), I don't think his wife surrounded by floating furniture would have been entirely in agreement with his priorities. Certain then that the water would come into the cottage, my mother and I began carrying everything we could lift upstairs. It was not long before the water was trickling under the front door and spreading over the floor. I can see my grandmother (Mother Ginny as she was known), standing in the fireplace holding her skirts up and enveloped in clouds of steam as the water put the fire out. We had three or four inches over the floor when there came a knock at the door. "Are you all right, Jane?" It was Stratton Long. "Yis, my booty, we're orlrite," she replied. But he opened the door. Outside, the water was three feet deep. He could be forgiven for not knowing the difference in levels but the result was astonishing. The wall of water bursting inwards wrenched the door out of his hands, tipped over a chest of drawers and sent ornaments in all directions. The cottage floor was covered with linoleum and the great surge that came in went under it. In the centre of the room was a pedestal table which rose up on a small hill as if a great animal was rising under it, and toppled over. Everything in the room then began moving around. Stratton waded through it and picked my grandmother up, no mean feat, and carried her to the stairs. He told me later that her backside was so huge that both his hands disappeared into it as he pushed her up the stairs.

Mother Ginny at Morston

My grandmother was built on a grand scale. Her knickers were so large that on the linen line they could sweep the ground. When she got older and had begun to shrink a bit they fell down a lot, mostly in the street or in the shop across the road. Once, following her and my mother along a hospital corridor, I saw them fall. She walked out of them and, hardly turning her head, spun her walking stick 180° and hooked them up. The stick continued its circle and, passing twelve-o-clock, they slipped off and into her voluminous handbag so neatly they could have been alive. I imagined them folding themselves up neatly inside. It was executed with a dexterity and precision quite unexpected in one unable to keep her knickers up. It seemed like a later development, but having had 14 children its possible she'd always had trouble keeping them up. Years before my time, the wooden seat of her outside privy had collapsed. She engaged one Ernie Allen, the unusually reluctant – in this case – local carpenter to make her a new one. Quite some time after having agreed to do it, he rather sheepishly reappeared, cap in hand, and after some beating about the bush confessed he had no idea how big to make the hole. "Oh don't you worry about that, my darlin'," she replied. "You just meak it up and I'll come round and sit on it. You can chalk round my arse."

It is amazing how much detail the atomic flash can burn into one's memory. While Stratton was pushing my grandmother up the stairs I noticed a flotilla of saucepans coming out of the pantry, like ducks, one behind the other in a neat convoy and in descending order of size. Stacked one inside the other they must have fallen over and drifted out in the same order. It all seemed unreal.

There was little more that could be done after Stratton left. Hoping it would not come any higher, we went to bed with the house beneath us full of water. I do remember worrying that having come up so much higher than it had ever done before, it might just continue rising. There seemed no reason why it should stop.

How different it would be today! Now we would be whisked off, willing or not, to a place of safety to be bossed around by people who enjoy wearing uniforms and delight in the opportunity to wield some authority. We would doubtless be given counselling, as good a way as any I can think of to erase the atomic flash. Trauma is part of life, and except in extremis it surely must be better and wiser to remember.

The morning brought great distress to my mother and grandmother. Almost all that my grandmother possessed was ruined. The deluge had left inches of mud over everything. Because I had been so praised for my efforts the night before, I willingly began to help clean up but I could tell that I was not wanted. I went out to inspect the damage elsewhere. The street was so choked full of tangle[1] and other rubbish that I couldn't get out through the gate and had to climb over the wall. Once again, just as on Mariner's Hill the day before, I knew I was witness to something extraordinary. With that came the realisation that I should try to remember as much as I could. I walked first to the top of Westgate Street to see how far the tide had reached. The street is slightly lower on the east side, and a finger of tide had extended further there. I have since heard anecdotal accounts of the tide that night reaching to the top of Westgate Street, but it didn't. I stood and fixed the highest point it reached in my mind and, while I cannot deny that my account is equally anecdotal, I will still offer it as the most accurate you will get.

West Corner where Duggy lived, now called Lady Bird Cottage, presents a gable end to the road. A low wall runs around the front in which there is a little gate. The last bits of tangle lay in the gutter exactly outside it.

I was joined by some other boys at that point, and it was a group of us that went around the quay. It was an amazing sight. In places, the tangle and rubbish was ridged up in great waves, splashed against the walls as if it were the sea itself, frozen at the height of its fury. Billy's Jane Hannah sat astride Quay House wall in a space she had made for herself. All one side of her was smashed in and she seemed beyond any hope of repair. The wall was eventually rebuilt but her shape remained, and is still just visible in the slightly different colour of the newer mortar.

The road was covered with tangle but among it was all sorts of other stuff – small household objects, pitifully meagre personal items that the owners would have been embarrassed to own up to, and hundreds of packets of cigarettes and playing cards from the Blakeney Hotel cellars. Many of the playing cards were loose and scattered around, giving the scene a very surreal quality as if it was all the result of some terrible game and they were the coda. Under all this mess lay dead freshwater fish, so many that people were being upended all over the place. A bigger surprise awaited us beyond the east sea bank. Topping it, we beheld a sheet of water stretching to the horizon. The fresh marsh was one vast lake with just a few posts and bushes breaking the surface. Blakeney Haven lay before us, the huge refuge that had once held a hundred-and-twenty ships during one storm, had been recreated for us by another.

Against the wider damage that night, Blakeney was quite fortunate. There was no loss of life as in Wiveton and Salthouse, and considerably less damage to property. Nevertheless, with all the mud, tangle and personal effects strewn around the streets, it was a dismal mess. I know a little of history's other rages and it is difficult from scant records and the quite different perceptions of disaster in times past to know with certainty how serious they were, but my instinct leads me to think that '53 was the worst tidal surge Blakeney has ever experienced.

1. Tangle is all the dead vegetation off the marsh, which accumulates at the end of summer and will build up over many months, sometimes years, before a big tide lifts it off and leaves it as a tideline.

9 Secondary School

Within a couple of weeks of the floods I began at Wells Secondary Modern. To have called any state school in Norfolk modern in the 1950s was an overstatement. Many would have qualified as secondary but few were modern. The school's ambitions for its pupils were not high – turning out boys for the land and girls for the scullery – and, with landowners dominating the board of education, that was slow to change. Against that background I was singularly fortunate in going to Wells. I have only happy memories of it. I was constantly in mischief, got the cane almost daily and, as that failed to work, spent most of my break time during my last year standing under the clock outside the headmaster's study, but it was worth it for the fun. There were a couple of gratuitously cruel teachers who threw compasses or hit you across the knuckles with the edge of a ruler, but there were others that even today would rate among the very best, and I was lucky to have two of them, Alan Drury and Bill Barnett.

Alan was the art teacher and Bill took history and occasionally art. Shortly after I arrived, a new timber building was erected to house three extra classrooms, and Alan Drury had the middle one. He was a mild, gentle character; so his classes were often unruly. If things got out of hand he would take the ringleader out into the lobby where he would raise his voice and pretend to be hitting him by banging his arm on the thin walls. From the classroom it sounded as if they were being killed, but he never laid a hand on us. It was touching, slightly embarrassing and clever. Most of us would pretend we had been hit when we went back into class. For a while at the start of the third year we had Bill Barnett for art, and in one lesson he asked us to paint something topical. The year was 1956. I'm not sure what else was going on but I decided to depict a scene from the Hungarian uprising, the centre-piece a tank with its barrel pointing out of the picture with a body draped over it and other bodies under the tracks. There was a lot of bright poster red splashed around and Bill Barnett thought it was terrific. He and Alan Drury then arranged for me to have extra periods of art. Each week we had double periods of gardening, woodwork and PE. First they arranged for me to have the woodwork as art, then the gardening, and after that, apart from the weeks before the annual sports, PE. I don't think the national android-creating curriculum we have today would accommodate that. Mostly I painted portraits of those in my class and was often pestered by other boys who wanted to get out of PE to be sitters. Those two years were very important for me, not just because of what I learned but also for the confidence that the faith those two teachers had in me gave in later years.

Me

Graham Walker

A few years ago Bill's wife commissioned me to paint something for him. I was so pleased to be able to do that, and equally pleased that it turned out well. I wrote some lines on the back thanking him and telling him what a wonderful teacher we all thought he was and how important he had been for me. That they were prepared to do this for me in spite of the mischief was remarkable. I hated authority and could see no reason why I had to call any of the male teachers 'Sir', or do things that made no sense. My response, was constant misbehaviour. It was mostly harmless but it must have

Alan (Crotchy) Smith

Ray Bayfield

been infuriating for the teachers. One example, which wasn't entirely harmless, involved a female teacher who I will call Miss Russell. Her legs, the visible part of which appeared quite normal, must have altered dramatically above the knees as they made an audible chafing sound as she walked. As I passed her on one occasion I mimicked the sound. She turned with amazing speed and hit me hard in the back of the neck, and I went down as if I'd been poleaxed.

I thought her reaction unequal to the crime and so laid in wait for a chance to repay her. Quite soon it came. All the children from the outlying villages had to line up in the school's front playground, ready to march down the drive to their buses. Flanking the drive was a wire and post fence, and beyond that a drop of two or three feet into a rose garden. I noticed Miss Russell, who was riding her bike down the drive, stop and get off. Perhaps remembering something she had forgotten, she leant her bike against the fence and walked back up to the school. It was a large sit-up-and-beg bicycle with old-fashioned brakes that had small calipers in the middle of the handlebars. I quickly found a few spent matches and used them to wedge the calipers open, which jammed both brakes on. The timing of what followed could not have been much worse for her, with a playground full of watching children. She came marching back, took up her bike, put her foot on the pedal and appeared to throw herself head first through the fence into the flower bed, where she lay sprawled face down in the roses, her large bottom protruding from the vegetation.

Our music teacher was a very well-made young lady who had a profound effect on all of us developing boys. In one class the boy next to me pointed down to show the effect she was having on him and she saw him. "Bayfield," she shouted, "get outside." He looked mortified and only slowly got up to walk out as if heading into a stiff head wind. Another boy, Lionel Hewitt, hid behind the piano and as she began to play got his hands in the back, gripping the strings and hammers, which gave her a Les Dawson style of playing. She was very unhappy about that and got one of the male teachers to cane him. Lionel was also the boy who, having been given the word 'seed' to fit into a sentence by the English teacher, wrote "I seed three ships a sailing, a sailing on the sea".

He went on to become a police inspector, and years later when I was coming off Brancaster beach at about 4.am in the morning after a night's netting, he was waiting with a team of officers on illegal immigrant watch. I was suddenly the centre of many bright lights and could see nothing. From the darkness came a voice saying "Yes, that's him, that's Godfrey Sayers," and my legs almost gave way.

Bill Barnett

Bill Barnett also rode a large sit-up-and-beg bicycle. Returning to school after lunch, he had the knack of being able to get off it and let it continue riderless. A group of first year C-formers would gather for the privilege of catching it and taking it to the bicycle rack. We moved them on one day and took their place. Bill arrived at speed, slid off the bike and let it run on, and we did the same, smiling innocently as it gathered speed and headed off down the playground to disappear into the vegetable garden. But, as I said, Bill was one of the good ones. He laughed as much as we did, though he did make us retrieve it. One of the male teachers wore a grey serge suit and, like Miss Russell, had a big rear end. We would powder chalk onto his chair, which always put two large round patches on his bottom. This caused huge amusement among the class but it never amused him. On one occasion he took a swipe at me. I ducked and the carry-through knocked poor Alan Smith, who was sitting next to me, out of his seat onto the floor. On another occasion I was asked to hold out my hand for the cane (all I had done was leave out part of the date at the top of a page) and he brought the stick down with such force that when I pulled my hand away it cut my exercise book in half.

When Bill was 80 his wife asked me to paint him a picture. I cherished the opportunity and made more effort with that painting than any other I have done. And on the back I expressed my gratitude for all that he done for me

My mischief was rebellion against being hit, even though it meant I got hit more. There are certainly problem schools today, but I feel sure that most children nowadays do not behave as we did. They have no reason to. They are not bullied or humiliated or subjugated as we were. Nevertheless, I was very lucky to have had those two excellent teachers. Without them my memories of that school would have been very different.

I went on to King's Lynn Tech. To begin with I went on the train from Holt and stayed with my aunt and uncle who managed one of the Sandringham estate farms near Great Massingham.

The college gambling club.

Then I went on to lodge with Graham Walker, who had been one of the mischief group in my class at Wells. Our first lodgings were not the best. The woman was clearly just doing it for the money. We had very little to eat and were expected to do chores when we came back in the evening. Graham remembers that one of these was cutting the hedge. Graham carefully cut his side while I went round to do the neighbour's side, where I cut it off just above the ground all the way along. It stood looking very good for a few days until the wind blew it over. We were moved on and I cannot remember whether it was because of our behaviour or because we complained about not getting enough to eat.

Our second lodgings were perfect. Mrs Chamberlain already had four other boys lodging, and looked after us as if we were her sons. Every day on my way between college buildings I would drop in for a cigarette. My time at Lynn was happy, and although reprimanded for customising the college uniform I had little trouble for the first year, passing my mock GCEs with good marks. But then my course was changed. At that time King's Lynn after dark was a battleground for Teddy Boys and American servicemen, and if there were none of them around the Teddy Boys, led by 'Blackie' Allen, soon found other victims. Making my way back to the lodgings from college late one evening I became one of them. But I had worked as a fisherman since I was nine and was strong and quick enough to look after myself. One of them got hurt and that got back to the college principal, who soon had me on the carpet. While I could genuinely claim self-defence, my assertive attitude and customised uniform did little to help. To cut this short my mother decided I should leave. My being there was stretching her meagre resources. If I had succeeded in passing further exams and achieved a university place there is no way I could actually have gone. Young people with my background seldom did.

I returned and began working full time as a fisherman and bait-digger. In those days both these occupations were very well paid, but I wanted to see the world. Within a year I joined the merchant navy and had four good years before I met my wife, fell in love, got married, and the adult part of my life began.

10 The Winter of 1963

On this coast the winter of 1963 was remarkable, not for its salt-laden gales or huge drifts of snow but for the prolonged intensity of the cold, cancelling out the Gulf Stream and freezing the east of England. It was relatively benign until early January, when a large anti-cyclone established itself over Scandinavia, setting up cold east to south-east winds which, although they brought little snow, blew constantly and with varying degrees of intensity until the end of February. The temperature stayed below freezing throughout, down to minus 15° at night and sometimes not much higher during the day. Everything froze, even pipes two feet underground. Very rarely is it cold enough in this country for the sea to freeze, but in 1963 there was a rim of ice along all the beaches, and in the harbours there were ice floes.

At that time I was digging with Harry Bishop. He was one of the most influential people in my entire life – quiet, scrupulously

honest and never deterred from any course he set himself. The weather was never bad enough to stop Harry, and so I and the others who dug with him went out too. Years later one of them had been digging out at Stiffkey on a filthy day. When he declined to join a group that was leaving early, he was told "Oh, we forgot you're one of the Harry Bishop-trained diggers". Although Harry was much younger than my absent father, he fulfilled the paternal role and set an example at a time when I needed it most. I don't believe I was born strong-minded – quite the opposite in fact – but the years spent working with Harry changed that. Staying the course no matter how rocky it may be doesn't always work out, but if it only works out half the time it is worth striving for. As these chapters unfold you will meet others who refused to turn back. It's a character trait among those who work this coast.

The effects of the intense cold came very quickly. As it set in, the tides were getting smaller. As each one ebbed, rafts of ice were left sitting on the sands until the whole harbour was thickly layered. As the tides began to make (get bigger), all this ice was shoved further up the harbour while more was being added on each ebb. This soon created mayhem. The whole harbour became choked with ice floes, some as big as cars and tilted at all angles. I took a rather cheap camera to record some of it but I could only take one or two pictures before the camera froze.

Talking to Harry recently, we put together what we could of one of those days. We were digging at Blakeney. There were four of us, and before setting off we stood looking at the channel. There was some discussion as to whether the sea could freeze as solid as fresh water at our latitude, so to find out Harry and I walked across to the other side. It took our weight easily. Further down the channel in the New Cut, all the mussel canoes were embedded up to their gunwales and could not be budged. It was at this point a few days later that the channel became so choked with ice that it formed a dam, preventing the tide from getting up to the quay. We passed some diggers who had gone a little earlier and had given it up. There was nowhere to dig, they said, and where the sand was not covered with ice it was as hard as the road. Traversing the ice field was certainly difficult, but of course none of this deterred Harry. The blocks of ice, although rough and jagged, were very slick on top and walking over them was treacherous. We all took a tumble at some point. After some distance we came upon one of the older diggers who had tried to cross a very large floe which dipped in the middle like an enormous bowl. He had slipped and ended up at the bottom of it and was unable to get out. Every time he tried he just slid back down He had been there a while and looked very cold. One of us was able to reach him with an extended fork and we got him out, but we wondered what would have happened to him if we had turned back with the others. I think eventually he would have realised that he could have used his fork as an ice pick. After setting him free we discovered that if we struck down hard with our heels they would make a break in the surface of the ice big enough to give purchase. After that we made better progress. That day we got a few worms by quickly digging where the tide was retreating – not many, but better than going home.

Me standing by an ice floe

As the weeks went by all the bait diggers except our small gang went on National Assistance. We didn't because we found a way to keep going. Either side of the harbour among the acres of spartina there are many shallow drains, none more than a couple of feet deep. We found we could cut the ice that covered these into pieces the size of paving slabs, lift them out and stack them alongside. Once this was done we would build dams of sand or mud across sections of the drain, bail the water out, dig the worms, let the water back through and then re-seal the dam and dig out the rest. It kept us warm and had benefits beyond our personal gain. It was a devastating winter for birdlife. Wading birds that depended on invertebrates were dying in their hundreds, but our small excavations served to save a few. Birds that would not normally have come within a mile of a human, like curlews, were almost under our feet as we dug, a very satisfying and rare privilege. This method of working served us well and we managed that way until the end of February when the thaw came.

11 Fishing With Stanley

Stanley with a couple of good fish

I was 24 when I began fishing with Stanley. He was in his early forties. Even then a reputation had grown up around his prowess. I say reputation, but it was more of a myth. More than once I heard him referred to as a 'fish master', though I've never really known what that means. It was as if Stanley's ability to catch fish owed something to the dark arts; that perhaps he hypnotised fish into the net. This amused him. He was happy for people to believe whatever they liked as long as they didn't try to copy us or get in the way.

There was nothing mysterious about Stanley's ability to catch fish. It was entirely down to his intelligence, imagination and a very individual approach to life. We fished the beaches along the coast from Titchwell to Walcott, using a method known as 'Drawing the Shore' walking in with a net and chest waders, and occasionally on steeper beaches like Cley, with a small dinghy. To transport our gear Stanley had built a barrow, made from a long and rather narrow tin bath (not unlike the one Pauline used) mounted on bicycle wheels with a length of metal rod bent into a handle, and a wooden foot so we could park it. The advantage of the bath was that in certain conditions it became amphibious. Netting for sea trout was not just a job. It was an adventure. There were so many unpredictable possibilities for excitement, like bringing a small dinghy ashore in large waves and hoping that you had collected up enough slack top line to let you get to the beach before the net pulled tight and dragged your stern under the next wave. We had to outwit the recreational netters who, although only doing it for fun and something good to put on the table, were frustrating our efforts to earn a living. One in particular, would sell his surplus and then call in on Stanley to tell him how good a price he got . We never used a torch. After years of working in the dark, your eyes adjust and you can see perfectly well on anything but the darkest cloud-covered night. The amateurs never realised that and were always putting on a laser show of torch beams, which told us their position but blinded them to ours. So many times we knew we were in for a good night because their excited shouting told us so, but they would fall quiet after we set in ahead of them. There were the things you were likely to see only if you spent many nights under the sky. On one night of thick cloud, something above the clouds (probably a meteor) flared with such intensity that it turned night into bright day, only for a few seconds but enough for us to see Scolt in the far distance and to leave us as blinded as if we had switched on a torch. The brilliant aurora borealis, wheeling and flickering with colours, took our breath away, UFO doppelganger light effects that would send the average nutter running for the phone. Then there was fog, usually in tandem with a calm sea, at least for a day or two[1.]

On one occasion we were fishing at Holkham on a perfect night; warm with a calm sea and a rising tide. It was my turn to pull and we quickly began catching fish. We had been having a lean spell, so we became excited at the prospect of a good catch. I cannot begin to tell you just how instantly and addictively exciting this can be. All else gets pushed aside. You think of nothing but fish, and the more you catch the more you want to catch. So when a sea fog rolled in we hardly noticed. It made little difference to our fishing, even though we knew we were working out along a sand bar. We kept catching fish, becoming ever more excited until we had fished our way off the end of the bar. Stanley called me in, and I found him and the barrow standing in a foot or so of water. "We could be in trouble here," he said. "We'd best get off quick".

We bundled the net into the barrow, fish, weed, gillies and all, and then looked around. There was nothing to see, just a flat calm sea, dense fog, and beyond that, darkness. The only clue was the barrow, facing along the sand bar as Stanley had left it, pointing west. So, turning south, we struck off, wading toward where we thought the shore must be. Slowly it got deeper until Stanley was over the tops of his thigh boots, then up to his waist, and soon to his chest. By then it was coming over the top of my chest waders.

At this point we stopped to ponder our position. We had been wading for a long time and both of us were wondering if we might not have walked in a circle – easily done in fog – and be heading back out to sea. However, we agreed that even if we had, we would still not know which way the shore lay, and so, resolved to continue straight ahead. We had noticed a number of times when pulling the barrow that we each had a tendency to tug in opposite directions, and so hoped this might have kept us straight. As we moved forward the water went on getting deeper until it was up to our necks and we were more or less on tiptoe. Stanley said he wished he had cut the corks off the net and put them around his neck to keep his head up, because like so many fishermen he couldn't swim[2.] By this time we were almost treading water and were very grateful for the barrow floating with us, which gave us something to hang on to. This terrifying ballet seemed to go on for an age before we finally touched ground and waded ashore, exhausted and very relieved to be on dry land. I remember thinking as we sat there that throughout the whole ordeal, Stanley lost neither his sense of humour nor the conviction that we would survive.

When conditions were right, and before they built the gas terminal, we often fished at Bacton. One night, apart from very thick fog, everything was perfect. We'd had several hauls and it must have been about 1.30 in the morning when we heard sounds up ahead. We guessed it had to be an angler. As Stanley went back out with the net, he quietly instructed me to leave the barrow and stay well back. With visibility down to less than ten yards, he disappeared in seconds. We proceeded slowly toward the lone angler. After we had covered about a hundred yards I heard a low moaning sound followed by a high, almost shrieking whine. I pulled a length of the net ashore and walked on to see what was afoot. When I got there I could tell from the marks in the sand that it was the angler – not just afoot, but like winged Mercury up the beach and gone as fast as his legs would carry him, while Stanley rolled around in hysterics. He had waded along silently, pulling the net until he judged he was opposite the angler and had then walked inshore toward him. He got it dead right and came

moaning out of the sea right in front of the poor man, who reeled in his line and fled. We followed his footprints up the beach and I swear they were ten feet apart. We wondered what his tale would be when he arrived home early to his wife. It's so easy to see how Black Shuck came into existence.

During the day in summer Stanley caught whitebait and sand eels in the harbour. He drove his old van along the meols[3] and out onto the island of high ground in Morston Marsh, which reduced the distance he had to carry his gear. After a haul he would shake out the small or damaged fish onto the sand, which the terns would then come and feed on. This happened so regularly and for so many years that generations of the birds knew him, but they didn't just know him, they knew his van and would come in their hundreds to meet him as he drove down. They would then stay with him all the time he fished, following him from place to place.

Stanley had a great sense of humour and an unflagging and often quite groundless optimism, but most of all a singularly individual and determined approach to life. He did not follow well-trodden paths. He chose his own direction and his own objectives, cut his own path to get to them and had the strength of character to overcome the obstacles that such choices inevitably brought with them. For me that sets him among the very best of men.

I have always believed that we are defined by our friends. So I consider myself very fortunate that, for almost a lifetime, I had Stanley as one of mine.

---

1. There is an old fisherman's saying that a fog brings on a swell. Even as a youngster I could not fathom the connection, but I was taking it too literally. While there is no way that the presence of fog could affect the sea state, the coincidence of the two happens too consistently for them to be unconnected. I think the explanation is this.

Foggy weather almost invariably coincides with an anti-cyclone which brings calm weather. The normal wave action in the North Sea varies from day to day, changes with the strength and direction of the wind and creates all sorts of sea states. But when the wind dies over the whole of it, as it does when there is a large area of high pressure, something different happens. The much larger seas of the North Atlantic, which run from west to east and sweep around the north of Scotland, are normally erased by winds from other directions. But now they begin to run uninterrupted down the North Sea and, after a few days, they reach our beaches. It takes a little time, so the first few days of fog will allow any seas to settle and some good fishing can be had. But after a bit swells begin to build. If the calm weather continues for any length of time, then really big seas can result.

3. This is based on the simple truth that ending up in the sea meant almost certain death, so why learn to swim and postpone the inevitable? These days the likelihood of rescue is so much greater; so – inshore at least – I think swimming might save your life.

4. Meols, now pronounced Meals is the term for the areas between arable land and that covered by the tide at its highest point such as that reached 1953 or 2014. It consists of gorse , Suaeda and coarse salt tolerant marsh grasses.

12 John Bean

As my children came along I needed a more reliable source of income, so I bought a one-ton van and set up a round selling cockles and mussels to fishmongers around Norfolk. The mussels came from my own beds and I gathered cockles from a good set I'd found at 'Wells Loo'. This is the name it is given if you live east of it. 'Stiffkey Loo' if you live to the west. If you don't live here at all it's Warham Sands. I pushed the cockles off on an old stripped-down moped; no seat, just a frame and wheels. The gear (bucket, rake, sieve etc.) was hung over the seat stem, and the sacks of cockles fitted into the crotch of the frame.

On a day of strong easterly winds and small tides, blowing sand ruled out any cockling; so I walked through East Hills. Coming out the other side, opposite Wells Lifeboat House, I discovered a terrific set of cockles high up under the Hills and sheltered from the blowing sand. This seemed like an answered prayer. The only problem was the distance I would have to push them off, almost twice the distance from the Low. But they were all I would get that day so I went back for my gear, only to discover that all but the tip of one handlebar had been buried by the sand. I dug it out and returned to gather what I could in the time remaining. The cockles were so plentiful that I managed to get most of my order with enough time to get off before dark. The journey back proved to be every bit as arduous as I had expected. Although the cockles were plentiful, it was clear that it would be a real test of stamina if I wanted to go on working from there. I decided to give it a try, and for a week or two I managed it. The last day was one of strong easterly winds and continuous snow. From where I was working, the distance back to the van, which I'd had to leave at the top of Chalk Road track at its junction with the coast road, was more than four miles. I had gathered four sacks, each of around 200kg, which completely filled the space between the handlebars and seat stem of the moped, making it difficult to reach over them and steer. I had shelter for a short distance around East Hills but it didn't last. Fortunately the sand was firm, if a little ribbed, so with head down into the blizzard I pushed on. Even in those conditions that stretch was relatively easy and I made good progress.

But I knew that ahead was a challenge that would test me to the limit. At a point where all the bait-diggers converged on their way off the marsh was a wide expanse of deep churned mud, bounded by creeks on either side. It was unavoidable and about a hundred metres across. I had to get through it in one attempt. To stop or even slow down would mean the bike sinking to the axles and me having to drag bags of clean washed cockles through soft mud. When I got there I rested for a while. Peering at it through the blur of snow, I wondered if it were humanly possible to do such a thing.

Once (to impress Judy, my then wife-to-be) I lifted a Mini with four youngsters in it out of soft sand at Wells Beach car park. This looked very much harder than that. Taking in as much oxygen as I could, I went for it. Halfway between a run and a trot, slipping and slithering, I shoved the moped along, knowing that the slightest easing of pace would leave me stuck. At the halfway point I could so easily have just stopped and given the whole thing up. But I had worked too hard for those cockles, so with my heart bursting I continued. I often think of that day now when cycling into a strong headwind – pedal, don't think about how far it is, just pedal and keep pedalling till you get there: a maxim for life. After an age I got through to firmer ground and could rest. Halfway back, I thought, and the worst is over. But it wasn't. Getting over the salt marsh still took a long time, the snow having made it so slippery. When I finally got off it was almost dark, although not too dark to see that Chalk Road was blocked with snowdrifts. I would have to go up the field on the sheltered side. As if to complete the day, under the snow this turned out to be ploughed. The moped just went in and stuck. At that moment my determination evaporated. I thought I'll just leave it all and come back tomorrow, but in such conditions I knew the cockles would freeze. So I took them all off, pulled the moped out of the soft soil and tried it with just one bag. Although difficult, this seemed to work. So, one bag at a time, I ferried them up to the halfway point. After this the track was just passable, so when I had completed the relay I loaded them all up again and struggled to finish the journey. By this time it was quite dark, but ahead I could see lights where I thought my van should be. When I got there I found my brother-in-law David waiting.

Judy had become so worried that she had asked him to come and look for me. I think he was as relieved to see me as I was to see him.

Provided the snow would let me deliver the cockles, I'd had a good day, but not one that was regularly repeatable – two bags possibly, maybe three, but four was too much and with orders increasing I needed another way. The obvious answer was to take a boat to Wells and just row across the harbour, but what to use? The mussel canoes were too big and heavy. Then I remembered a small dinghy that Beano sometimes used, and went to see him. There were cockles and orders enough for the two of us, and he willingly agreed to join me. The ten-foot, flat-bottomed ply dinghy was perfect, easy to lift and carry and, as we were to discover, very seaworthy. It changed the job completely. I no longer came home exhausted and I had the company of a good friend.

The winter went by easily and happily, with cold but calm weather. Then in the space of a day it changed. It began cold with a fresh north-east wind, and we got across early to bring the dinghy and gear up close to where we were working. The wind steadily increased during the day, bringing snow, but we worked hard and when the tide returned we had gathered 18 pecks of cockles, 150 kg. By then the wind was blowing hard; so we decided that three sacks would be enough. We dragged them and the dinghy as far as we could to meet the tide, and in retrospect there is no doubt that this saved our lives. But we were still left with a long and by then frightening crossing. Beano insisted on taking the oars and I didn't argue. With us, the cockles and the gear, the dinghy was well down, and with so little freeboard we knew that once we pushed off we were committed. There would be no coming about. We would have to press on. We quickly lost the shelter of East Hills and were in seriously rough water for such a small craft. In a situation that turned entirely on Beano's rowing, our position relative to the waves had to be kept perfectly straight and balanced. Pull just a little too hard and the bow would have buried. Too slow and the next following sea would have been aboard. As we progressed and the waves got bigger, the margin for error got smaller. I was frantically baling, and he with the wind and snow in his face pulling for all he was worth, when suddenly he looked

That Beano stare

straight at me, grinned, and said, "Whatever you do, don't look behind. You'll shit yourself." Clobbered up with doppers (waterproof oilskins with hoods) and thigh boots, we wouldn't have stood a chance if we'd sunk. Rolling on in such turbulence, it seemed impossible that we could make it, each wave flinging us forward and threatening to push the bow under - but we did. Hitting the shore we both leapt clear, and as we did so the next wave washed in and filled the dinghy to the gunwales. For those of you who know the sea, that will tell how delicately Beano hedged the inevitable.

During the years after this I gradually moved up from a small van to a lorry, expanding my wholesale mussel business, taking larger consignments to the Midlands and bringing shoe machinery from the BU[1] back to Norwich. Furniture removals and general haulage also became an important part of it, but these things took me away from the coast and so are not part of this story. After a decade I took the lorry off the road and it became the gallery that stood on Blakeney Carnser for 38 years but now operates from my garden. I then came back to bait digging in the winter.

1. British United Shoe Machinery

If you look at an Ordnance Survey map of Blakeney Point, you will see tucked behind its penultimate lateral arm a bay called Stanley's Cockle Bight. Before Stanley (Webster) started cockling there it was just called The Bay. It was a very fertile spot for both cockles and lugworms, which coexisted in such profusion that Stanley was worried that a gang of bait diggers would find the lugworms and dig the cockles in getting at them. So he asked me if I would go and dig behind him as he cockled. With worms so abundant I was more than happy to do that, although it required some cunning and minor deceit to pull off, as for several months I had to get out there and back every day without being seen.

I was digging for Harry Bishop at the time, and decided to explain the situation to him first. He would then ring me to let me know how many to get, so I could avoid the rest of the diggers. The bait was so plentiful in The Bay that I could leave an hour after the gang had gone and still be back an hour before they returned. Not being seen was more difficult. I would dodge out over Morston Marsh, keeping down in the creeks as much as possible, then skirt round the end of the Pit and make my way down through the dunes.

Beano was winter warden on the Point at this time, so keeping it from him was impossible. He soon told me he knew what I was doing, but although he was digging part-time himself he never came near. I managed one whole season of the best digging I'd had as Stanley harvested the largest and most plentiful area of cockles ahead of me. Once these were all cleared I told Beano he was welcome to join me if he liked, and from then on we went together, often going early and having breakfast in front of the fire in the Lifeboat House. The Lifeboat House gave this period an almost nine-to-five feel, as we could go back there on bad days and have our lunch in front of the fire too.

I remember one day which I think summer users of the Pit would find difficult to believe. We were going over just after high water on a large spring tide with a westerly force 9 blowing right down the harbour. "I don't fancy this in a dinghy," Beano said. "I think we'll take Sea Urchin." (This was his biggest ferry boat and only a little smaller than Snow Goose, which I had used for fishing parties.) But we had no idea how rough it was going to be.

When we got to the mouth of Morston Creek, the tide against wind created a slog that was unbelievable. It was unsafe to put our nose out even in a ferryboat, waves eight feet high and troughs deep enough for a 35-foot barge to sit in. I have never seen the Pit any rougher than this. It was like the open sea. We dug together happily in the Bay for a month or two until Beano's brother Grumpy, his uncle Kitch and Mike Bennett joined us. And so began a couple of the happiest years of my life which, considering I hated bait-digging, is saying something. Mike had been a teacher in his native Nottinghamshire and had taught for some years at Blakeney School before making the unusual choice of becoming a bait-digger. Like Beano he was a keen wildfowler and had the same down-to-earth sense of humour that we all shared. We were a like-minded group who were happy in each other's company. We got across to the Point, squeezed into the same dinghy that had kept Beano and me safe across Wells Harbour. Sometimes in strong winds I wondered if we would make it, but we always did.

These extracts from the address I gave at his memorial service should give a clearer idea of Beano's character. It begins with some words by Robert Macfarlane. From his book 'The Wild Places' Published by Hamish Hamilton

In appearance; slight, weather beaten and tough;
In manner, sharp, generous, mischievous.
His physique, like his language, compact and wiry, capable of reach and strength.
Physically, whipped tight, made of hawser and halyard wire, but his character full of flex.
On the water passes in and out of moods of intense concentration, moments when you cease to be with him,
Whose endings are marked by a quick grin, a register shift, or a sudden impiety.
He doesn't take well to fools or frauds.
At first meeting you would be gauged, appraised, quickly read. Eyes moved up and down over you. Giving the same sense of apprehension as when stepping through an airport scanner.

That in essence is Robert Macfarlane's description of a Hebridean seaman, but it's a perfect fit for Beano. I was tempted to add the word fearless, because in his everyday life Beano was quite fearless; but of course fearless seamen are reckless seamen, and he certainly wasn't one of those.

1. *Slight, weather beaten and tough, his physique, like his language, compact and wiry, capable of reach and strength. Whipped tight yet full of flex.*

Characteristics shaped by, and essential for, survival in the harsh and unforgiving environment we have here. But of course Beano did more than survive. He thrived. This was his element, his world, and he was master of it. On the water, on the Point, on the marsh, on the shore, through all of these he moved with a sure and certain grace. Actions and manoeuvres that for most would require a fair amount of mental rehearsal and preparation, he executed with a smooth, almost casual unselfconscious ease. Seemingly without thinking, second nature. Which of course it was, but that tells only part of it. That oneness doesn't just fall from the sky. To be in harmony with such a complex and unpredictable environment needs some very particular skills.

Natural ability; a talent if you like, and if you've been to sea with someone who doesn't have it, someone who always seems to have their backside in your face at the worst possible moment, you'll know how important that is.

An agile intelligence – to be able to think a way through a confused and frightening situation that you have never encountered before. And no matter how much experience you may have, you will still get those. Then of course experience itself, experience which in Beano's case extended back to childhood. These attributes are rarely matched. There are plenty who have some of them, but only a few who have them all; and even fewer who have them to the degree that Beano did. There are one or two in this church who do. But only one or two.

2. Passing in and out of moods of intense concentration, moments when you cease to be with him, the endings of which are often marked by a quick grin, a register shift, or sudden impiety.

Here I recounted the crossing of Wells Harbour.

3. Little tolerance for frauds or fools. Gauged, appraised, and quickly read. Like stepping through an airport scanner. Then the green light. Genuine. Nothing hidden.

I suspect that most of you at some time or other will have faced the unwavering stare of the John Bean scanner, and only you know if you got the green light or not. Beano's judgment of people was second to none. He fielded the best prat detector you'll ever come across. He could spot what he called a half-sixer a mile off – a half -sixer being someone who isn't what they pretend to be, or is not what they think they are. For the fools, well that would be the sort of person we see more and more of these days, who out on the water set themselves very low standards of seamanship, which they then fail to live up to, usually just in front of you and when there is no time or room for manoeuvre. And the frauds of course wouldn't just be detected. Often they'd be exposed. I think Doris Temple (The fiesty landlady of the Anchor pub) schooled him in the last bit. But as with the wind and the water, his astuteness went beyond people. I relied on his judgment many times. He was the one person I knew who could give me an inside track; he could always see through the smokescreens of bureaucratic gobbledygook thrown up by the agencies who have now assumed the authority to determine how we live here, to get at the core of what was being hidden or planned. No-one pulled any wool over Beano's eyes. Thinking of this, and how consistently good at it he was, I tried to come up with a word to describe it. Wisdom? Insight? Prescience? Whatever it was, he was never wrong.

So those of you here today who got the John Bean green light might want to sit up, stand up a little bit straighter; feel a little better about yourselves. Because there is no doubt you were never more shrewdly judged.

13 Line Squall

During the years I fished with Stanley at night I was taking fishing parties out for Stratton Long (the man who let the floodwater into my grandmother's house) during the day. If we'd had a hard night and I had to leave on the tide at 7.30am, it could make for a long twelve hours at sea. We were expected to do all we could to make sure the anglers caught fish, but I was lucky in that several of the groups I took out were old hands who could look after themselves. This allowed me to have the odd catnap on one of the side thwarts, but catnaps they always were. Being so far out to sea in an open boat, a weather eye was always needed. There were three boats that we used for fishing parties, two of them ancient ship's lifeboats called White Swan and Snow Goose – I always took Snow Goose – and a new purpose-built boat called Ptarmigan, which Michael Taylor (my brother–in-law) usually took.

The anglers' main prey were the bigger fish, mostly tope[1] and skate, which were found further offshore around and beyond the Bell Buoy (called the Bellman, about six miles off). On this day I had a group of five young airmen. They came equipped to catch skate, and the Bellman was our destination. With novice anglers I had plenty to do helping them to fish efficiently, and we were having a good day until about mid afternoon when Michael, who was fishing just a few hundred yards away, called out to me. He was pointing to the sky off to the southwest, where a belt of dark cloud was boiling off the land toward us: a line squall[2]. Line squalls are often caused by weather fronts coming through, and in a very short time can bring very strong winds and rain. Michael indicated that we should go. Of the five airmen, four had caught a skate and the last one got a fish on his line right at that moment. Skate have a habit when hooked of hanging onto the bottom, and it can take 20 minutes to half an hour of constant hauling to tire them to the stage where they can be pulled in. Even then they are like underwater kites and don't come easy.

As the wind arrived and the seas picked up, I told him to cut his line. They all then pleaded with me to give him a chance to catch his skate, which stupidly I agreed to. He persevered, but as the boat began to pitch more violently it became difficult for him.

It looked as if he would never get it clear, but after twenty frantic minutes he finally got his prize. But valuable time had been lost. The lift from the increasing waves did help me get the anchor free, but I had to hand the rope over to a couple of the airmen to pull it up while I dashed back to the tiller to keep the boat's head up into the weather. But it didn't work. They couldn't do it, and shouting instructions from the tiller had no effect. I also realised that if they ever did get it clear of the water it would swing around and smash into the hull. I needed to be in two places at once. I put one of them on the tiller with a quick brief on what not to do, and went forward and got it aboard. Even before I had finished we were falling away into the troughs as he had failed to keep our head up. By this time the seas were becoming short, steep and dark with streaks of foam running down their fronts. Heading directly for the shore would have meant driving straight into them, being lifted high by one and thrown down hard into the next. Snow Goose was too old and frail to last long doing that, so I set an angled course for Weybourne and for a while managed to wriggle my way over and through the worst of it without putting her to the test. As the seas got bigger and windblown spray reduced visibility, I got caught by three very big ones, the last of them lifting me high. As Snow Goose plunged down I heard a loud crack and my arm was wrenched as the entire rudder, complete with the tiller, was torn loose and thrown high above me to come crashing down into the boat like an enormous axe. At least holding it had given me some control over where it came down, so no airmen were injured.

Everything then became chaotic. The boat rolled violently as it lay broadside on to the seas with five men who, while they may have been able to fly were completely unable to keep their feet. They were sliding around on the floor, some on their backs, some on their fronts along with the fish they'd caught, the slime from which was making the whole thing much worse. Whether or not Stratton had foreseen such an event I don't know (I doubt anyone would have had the imagination to foresee what I was witnessing that day), but he'd had the foresight to equip each of the boats with two old oars from the last Blakeney lifeboat.

The Mary converted into a fishing boat

These were long, broad-bladed and heavy enough to serve my purpose. I managed to get one over the side and secured to the starboard side quarter post, and with this as a primitive rudder I managed to get her head back into the wind. But it was still a losing battle. I called two of the airmen aft and got them on the oar while I got the other one over the port side and put two more on that. I then varied the speed of the engine and we were underway again. But we were not getting any closer to land. We were no longer taking in water over the side and were cresting the waves without too much stress on the boat, but we were slowly being carried out to sea and into increasingly rough water. This strenuous juggling continued for a while until to my huge relief I saw another larger boat coming toward us. It was Robin Bishop in the Mary (formerly the Winterton lifeboat). He came up on our lee side and I told one of the airmen to undo the anchor and throw him the rope. He managed to get it undone but couldn't throw it far enough for the Mary to pick up. Again I needed to be in two places at once. The airmen seemed to have got the hang of the oars, so I dashed forward and managed to get a line to them. I let as much out as possible to reduce the snatch such big waves would subject it to, and we were in tow and heading for shore. Knowing how ancient Snow Goose was, Robin went gently, and having such a large heavy boat ahead reduced the wave action for us. I was able to hold position using just one oar and I slowly began to realise that we were safe. The Mary had made her last rescue. I vividly recall how frightened I was during this misadventure but am reassured in the knowledge that I wasn't so frightened that I couldn't do what was necessary to stop the boat from being rolled over. This is the third account in this book of my having looked the dark angel in the eye and having him blink first. But I am by no means unique. Most of those who go to sea in small boats would be able to tell similar tales. While they accept such risks as part of the job, they are nevertheless changed by them. Thereafter they have a different perspective on life. John Bean, Stanley Webster (sunk twice in the Atlantic convoys) and Graham Walker, who you will hear about later, typify the kind of men that result. It doesn't necessarily make anyone more courageous but it does underwrite a calm pragmatism about death. You are no longer afraid of being afraid. It gives a different perspective on risk and an undisguised contempt for those in today's society who define it.

---

1. A species of ground shark growing to about six feet in length. Postscript: A few years ago at Hewitt's boatyard I told this tale and added that steering with an oar was both difficult and not entirely effective. To which a local clever dick responded with. "I'm not sure that's right. After all, the Vikings managed to get all the way from Norway to here using them". David Hewitt instantly replied: "Ah yes, but they were trying to get to America."

2. Line Squalls are usually associated with cold fronts which are the leading edges of cooler air masses, hence the name "cold front". They have stronger temperature changes during the autumn and spring. Temperature changes associated with cold fronts can be very dramatic. When cold fronts come through, very strong winds can occur with heavy rain that indicates that the cold front is passing. The effects from a cold front can last from hours to days. The air behind the front is cooler than the air it is replacing and the warm air is forced to rise, so it cools. As the cooler air can t hold as much moisture as warm air, clouds form and rain occurs.

14 Excavations

From my childhood in Blakeney I'd heard tales of lost tunnels, some from the church, some from the Carmelite Friary but all ending in what is called the Guildhall on the quay. As children we often played in and around the Guildhall, where in the south-east corner we discovered a small dark square space – hardly a room, but more like the base of a stairway that had a deep hole in the wall and floor. None of us was brave enough to go into it, so we didn't know how far it went. I have looked in there since and can see no trace of it, but English Heritage carried out extensive works in the 1950s and may have filled it in. I remember hearing Will

Watch tell someone that as a young man he made his way at least 20 yards into a tunnel that led south from that corner. For a few years Mike Bennett, Beano and I would meet once a week, either at the Anchor in Morston or at the King's Arms in Blakeney. When it was the King's Arms we would often sit with Archie Bedwell, who had been a builder all his life in Blakeney and had some fascinating tales to tell. One evening we were talking about tunnels and the many stories that have come down about them, and he recalled repairing a wall in a garden behind the last of the row of cottages that run along the top of Mariner's Hill, and having a large hole open up under its foundations. He climbed down into it and was certain it was a tunnel running in the right direction to have come from the Guildhall. I was little sceptical because I remember when the White Horse car park just across the road caved in to reveal what looked like a tunnel but which turned out to be the cellar of a house that had once stood there.

Mike Bennett

But I also remembered the story of the highway-widening scheme by Fiddlers Hill on the Binham to Warham road, where the bones of a man and dog were unearthed. They were later dated as Bronze Age, but the legend* that had pinpointed a man and a dog under that hill had come down as Chinese whispers over 3,000 years. Perhaps there was a kernel of truth in the tunnel stories too. The three of us agreed that we would investigate Archie's tale and try to follow up any other tunnel stories to the point where, to our satisfaction at least, they were either proved or disproved.

We knew the owners of the cottage where Archie had worked, and took him there to show us where the tunnel was and also, we hoped, to stimulate the owners' interest sufficiently to allow us to dig. It did and they did. We carefully removed the turf and dug down, making a very big hole. But we didn't find any sign of a tunnel. We gave Archie the benefit of the doubt, concluding that the years had clouded his memory.

Having no other clear course of action, we decided that we would project the line to the south east, the direction in which Archie had said the tunnel ran, and see if there was anywhere else we might dig. The Cooke family, who owned the large house called

Richard Newton

the Friary just behind Mariners Hill, had quite a large orchard about a 150 yards along that line. Knowing Hereward Cooke quite well, I felt sure he would let us dig. I was working with Richard Newton at that time. Richard is a joiner and cabinet-maker who lived in Cley. When I told him what we were going to do, he said he knew of a diviner who might be able to focus our search. This man eventually came along and methodically walked the entire site. We hadn't told him anything other than that it was a tunnel we were looking for. He got regular drops of his divining rod in a line across the orchard that corresponded well with where a tunnel might be. He then let us have a go and (perhaps not surprisingly) we got even better results. This fired us up to dig and we ended up with an enormous hole. Richard had become the fourth member of the gang and we soon got down to solid chalk. This was where we should have stopped but, enthused by the divining results, we continued on down. We ended up with an Olympic-sized swimming pool but no tunnel or anything else of the slightest interest. I did think it odd that the diviner got a line corresponding exactly to the line we all thought a tunnel might follow. Perhaps he was divining our minds.

It seemed we'd come to a dead end. But then we got hold of some aerial photographs of the village and surrounding area, and these did prove interesting. While they showed nothing in the orchard where we'd been digging or anything else in Blakeney, they did show a clear line running across a field from Wiveton Hall to the junction at the bottom of Cley Hill, where Leatherpool Lane meets the A149 coast road. Sadly, lines that show up clearly on such photographs are very much more difficult to find on the ground, and the first exploration of the area was disappointing. But we went back, and along with Mike and Beano I quartered the field that the line crossed. The coast road would not have existed at the time of any tunnel (put in after the Glaven Valley was closed off in 1820), so Richard looked among the trees on the landward side of the coast road, and it was he who made the discovery. It was just a hole in the ground, not big enough to climb into but revealing some very ancient stonework that curved over to form part of what looked like the roof of a tunnel. We tried to open a way in but it was clear that it would have to be properly excavated. The land was then owned by a woman who I knew would be supportive. Although none of us had ever been on an archaeological dig, we knew enough to not just carelessly blunder in. The opening Richard had found had been filled with Victorian rubbish, most of which had long rotted away to leave just glass jars and bottles. Once these were removed we proceeded more judiciously, sieving and inspecting the spoil with more care. The more material we took out, the more like a tunnel it became. A small niche was revealed that looked purpose-built for a lamp or perhaps a candle, and some other, larger Romanesque arched recesses. Our initial digging had been in an inland direction, so we were disappointed when we cleared material at the north end and found a wall. It had another interesting recess built into it, but this rather dented the idea that it might be a tunnel.

Ronald Beresford-Dew

Around this time the property was sold to Professor Ronald Beresford Dew, and on that day I met another of the seminal people in my life. He was passionate about history and archaeology. He was and still is passionate about everything. The interruption of his studies at Cambridge by the second world war didn't prevent him on his return from very quickly (a two-year course accomplished in six months) becoming qualified as a barrister and then as a chartered accountant. He was quickly head-hunted to work for a company that reorganised engineering businesses, a subject on which he lectured at Manchester University, where eventually he was to become an emeritus professor. He was particularly successful in reorganising the car division of Rolls Royce, which required him to spend some time in the USA. There he became very impressed with their business schools and resolved to found one in Britain. As always seems to be the case in this country, it was an uphill struggle and there was a lot of pressure for the first one to be in London. Eventually two were founded – one in London and the other at Manchester. All the business schools that have followed have been based on those first models. He could hardly contain his excitement at what we had found. I could see that he was just bursting to get involved, but he didn't.

There are very few people like Ronald in the world. With his flair for organisation and enthusiasm for archaeology, how could he resist taking charge? Most people with his passion would have jumped in. But Ronald was different. We agreed that I would go and see him every couple of weeks and update him on whatever we had found, and that between us we would agree the way forward. The idea of bringing in the Norfolk Archaeology Unit, for example, was discussed and agreed by both of us. They were very keen to see what we had found. Dr Andrew Rogerson was sent out to meet us and he supported the way we had been working.

Shortly after they became involved we found a small piece of pottery under the base of one of the walls which they identified as 'Green Ware' and dated it circa 1250. Because it was found under the wall it suggested that the building was probably of the same date. Andrew thought it was the undercroft of a large house, similar but smaller in scale to the Guildhall in Blakeney or – because it fronted what then would have been a large tidal estuary – a fortification. When we had dug along the main wall for 15 metres we came to another wall at right angles, which suggested that we had revealed one end of a square or rectangular structure. This was a problem. To uncover any more of it we would have to remove a large mature tree. Ronald would, I'm sure, have agreed to this, though it would have been a task beyond us. We were very keen to excavate the whole site, but the removal of such a magnificent tree seemed too high a price to pay. We decided to shore up the roof we had exposed, clear up the site and call it a day. Always supportive, always enthusiastic, Ronald, who at the age of 94 still climbs three flights of stairs each day to use his computer, remains one of my dearest and most supportive friends.

---

1. For a wager a fiddler walked the length of a tunnel, which was rumoured to run from Walsingham to Binham. (As sound cannot easily penetrate the ground, this never made much sense. I doubt you'd hear Pink Floyd playing underground.) He took his dog with him, and his fiddling stopped when he got to Fiddler's Hill. Which is not on a line from Walsingham to Binham either, but the information that the remains of man and dog were under that hill came down intact through three millennia.

It was during the clearing up of the dig that the machine we brought in to level the spoil heap broke the main sewer pipe from Blakeney. While instructing the driver, I noticed that a tree some distance away kept swaying in time with the machine's blade. I stopped him but it was too late. The ground heaved to one side and a dirty tide poured out. The driver quickly made a dam to stop it from filling the dig, and diverted it into a natural basin behind a wall flanking Leatherpool Lane. Directly across the road lived Mr and Mrs Digby who, while this was all going on, walked past giving me her usual friendly wave and greeting of "Good morning, boys". By then the sewage was mounting higher and higher up the wall which was opposite their double gate entrance. I imagined Mr Digby contentedly sitting in his deckchair in the garden reading the newspaper as the wall gave way. I could see their gates bursting inward and him being swept away on a tsunami of sewage. Instructing the, by that time, quite panicked digger driver to create a channel to take the pressure off the wall, I rushed down to Richard's to phone Anglian Water. It took quite a while for them to get organised but eventually a fleet of tankers began going past every few minutes, taking the sewage away from the Blakeney pumping station to the plant further up the valley. This went on all day because the broken pipe proved to be obsolete and they had nothing with which to repair it. I asked the manager how much it would all cost, and when he told me I almost made my own contribution to the problem. It would run into at least six figures, he said, with far more enthusiasm than I thought appropriate.

Fortunately the script – as usual – was adjusted. George Curtis, father of my friend Mike (of whom more later), who had some sway with Anglian Water, remembered where such pipe could be found, and the problem was solved. It was also he who managed to get us off the six-figure cost of the repairs. When I asked him how he did it, he just said that he told our story at the meeting and it caused so much amusement they decided to let us off. I don't for a moment think it was that easy.

15 Effluent among the Affluent

I have worked as an artist for 40 years, and a similar length of time on local councils and advisories, but it is this incident that will be inscribed on my gravestone. This may be a good reason for leaving it out, but a better one for putting it in. It has grown so out of proportion over the years that perhaps the horse's mouth version should be given somewhere.

For at least eight years leading up to the 1980s the sewerage system around the quayside at Blakeney had been overflowing at peak holiday times. At its worst, rivers of raw sewage were running across the road and into the quay. From enquiries I had made, it seemed clear that the main cause of this was the Blakeney Hotel's lack of fat traps, which had allowed grease from their kitchens to congeal in the main sewer. As I cycled back around the quay from my gallery for lunch, I had to lift my feet as I passed through a wide river of raw sewage pouring across the road, and could see at least a dozen children, most of them without shoes, gilly-catching while the stuff ran between their toes into the quay. It seemed like the last straw. How much worse could it get without someone doing something about it? I was reminded of my grandmother's story of the death of an aunt I never knew, who caught typhoid from swimming in the quay, back in the days when the sewer emptied directly into it. I also remembered an entire winter's loss of income when Leicester Health Department condemned all our mussels because of E.coli. Over lunch I resolved to make a protest. My first thought was to collect a bucketful of the stuff and take it to North Norfolk District Council's offices in Cromer. But the thought of driving so far with a bucket of shit in the car seemed like an irresistible invitation for fate to provide an emergency stop. In any case it was the hotel that was at fault, so I decided to take it to them.

With a bucket and a small hand brush, I returned to the gallery. It was still pouring across the road, so I was easily able to collect a good bucketful where it was cascading over the edge of the quay. I included a colourful mix of toilet papers to ensure that nobody would be in any doubt as to what I had in the bucket, and went into the hotel. There were quite a number of people in the foyer and a few suitcases standing around. I asked for the manageress, and when she appeared I said something along the lines of, "The owners of this hotel seem quite content to let sewage run across the road if it's well away from their door. Perhaps they will see the matter differently if it's inside the door." And then, using the well-practised mussel-washing technique, threw the contents of the bucket in a grand arc across the carpeted foyer. This livened the place up no end. Squealing women clutched their skirts, some made a bolt for the door and others just froze on the spot. I got a pretty good spread and also a few suitcases, which was a pity because it wasn't the fault of the guests. The manageress then tried to prevent me leaving by standing in front of me, arms held back and pushing her ample chest out to make a barrier. This was an unexpected bonus, which only served to stiffen my resolve. She eventually gave up, peeled off to one side and let me go.

Later that afternoon a police inspector I knew from Cromer called at the house. And although I clearly set out my reasons for my action, and the results I hoped would follow, he still kept saying "but why did you do it"? Since then, mostly through my dealings with local authority officers and the like, I have come across many like him – people who are completely unable to see subtext. They also lack a sense of humour. It is a literalism bordering on autism, and they all seem to end up in the public sector. I duly went to court on a criminal damage charge, pleaded guilty and was fined £50. I subsequently received far more than that from friends and supporters. I returned the money to all who would take it, but still ended up with a profit of £35. I had expected to be taken to court and to be found guilty and fined, and I had hoped for the publicity it got, but people's generosity was a surprise. Soon after that, Dyno Rod vans appeared and the pipes around the quayside were cleaned out. Quite a few years after all this, as chair of the National Trust's management committee, I had a meeting with the newly-appointed regional superintendent for Anglian Water. As the introductions were made I noticed a flicker in his eyes. As we then walked on in conversation, I queried his reaction and was told with a smile that, being new to the job, he had boned up on all the bumf relating to this area and was amazed at how many times my name came up. He then went on to say that he was sure I would be surprised to learn that after my actions Anglian Water had put pressure on the Environment Agency to prosecute Blakeney Hotel for not having fat traps, and that they were eventually fined £3,000. That of course did not find its way into the papers.

There was a further incident that brought a smile to his face, and that chillingly had crept into my head during my trial. Standing in court, I remembered what had happened with the dig and suddenly had this terrible vision of the prosecution saying that damage done to the main sewer by me 18 months before had been the real cause of the sewage backing up and overflowing into the quay. Later on in the afternoon of that day, I had tea with Martin Ryle and told him the story. "If it will make you feel any better," he said, "I'll tell you one." Apart from being a brilliant scientist, Martin was a pacifist and had worked alongside Alfred Jodrell on

radar during the war. They were on the point of a breakthrough that Martin felt certain could shorten the war and, being so passionate about it, was charged with the task of persuading Whitehall to provide the money to pursue it. After meeting with a succession of people he ended up on the opposite side of a desk to a man he knew was going to say no. These individuals, and I've met them too, exist in most bureaucratic systems and rise up through the hierarchy by keeping their heads down. If they play it safe and say no to everything put in front of them, they avoid black marks and so rise to become a thrombosis in the system. Martin knew he'd got one of these. It was clear that no matter what he said, this man was never going to say yes. Nevertheless, he continued to make his arguments as powerfully as he could, but while doing so pretended to be fiddling with a large bottle of ink on the desk. When the man eventually did say no, he threw it all over him. Its the Irish in us!

16 The 78 Storm

Blakeney Quay showing Red House

When rain comes from the south-west, it seldom lasts more than two or three hours, hence rain before 7 clear by 11. When it rains from the east or north-east, it can often go on all day or sometimes for a couple of days. On this day it began raining early in the morning and continued all day, getting much harder during the afternoon, with large flakes of snow mixed in and the wind strengthening all the time. I'd been working all day with Richard Newton in Cley, and when I came home it was screaming. Because it was from the north-east, I wasn't sure how much it would put on the evening tide. About ten past seven I took Judy and the children to have a look. It was already into Westgate Street and up to the King's Arms yard, with nearly an hour-and-a-half to go until high water. I took everyone home, put on my thigh boots and went back. By then the water was a good twenty metres further up the street. The King's Arms had managed to get their flood boards in, but as I arrived they gave way, almost in slow motion it seemed. The boards parted like gates, allowing a mass of tangle and detritus to flow like lava into the yard. A window left open was reached by the water in just a few minutes and was then quickly shut. I doubted it would much affect the outcome.

Mike Curtis, who you will meet later, then arrived and asked if I would go with him to put the flood boards in for Red House. We got buffeted and soaked as we struggled to get there against the waves, with the water coming over the top of my thigh boots. When we arrived it was completely dry around the entrance where the flood boards were to go, but we were still too late. Red House stood in a lake about two feet deep. The water had come up through the drains. We made our way through into North Granary, where the water was coming up through the toilet like a geyser. It was hitting the ceiling despite having come round an S-bend. This was the legacy of a more ancient sewerage system installed in the days when they had run everything into the quay. There was little we could do, and coming back we stood for a bit and watched the waves crashing against the front of the hotel, one of those sights that imprints itself on the memory.

The tide eventually reached up Westgate Street to the The Pightle, a small cottage about halfway up. I went back to Red House with Mike next day and it was a terrible mess. Around full tide I went to Salthouse. I had no idea what to expect but, thinking it could be bad, I took the inland route over the heath and approached down Cross Street. It was surreal. I may just have picked a quiet moment but I didn't see a single person or vehicle, no life anywhere and no water on the road, just the continual howl of the wind and the banshee screams of the flood siren on the marsh. I imagined everyone cowering in their homes waiting for the worst, but in all likelihood those most in danger had retired to the village hall or friends' houses on higher ground. Realising how quickly the water would come in should the beach be breached, I drove quickly along to the Post Office corner, up the hill and away. Eerie.

The next morning I went to Bard Hill, high above, to see that the beach had indeed been breached in three places and the road was under water. It must have happened soon after I left. After lunch we took the children out along Cley bank to the beach to see the damage. The sea bank was breached in two places and at

other points which quite clearly how these earth banks are breached. Rather than giving way in large sections, as many people suppose, it appears to be a more erosive process. Waves lapping onto the top of the bank at a low point start water trickling over in small rivulets. These create gullies which, as the volume of water increases, turn into channels, then cuttings, then small breaches that quickly become major ones, all of which would happen in a quite short time. The beach wasn't as badly knocked about as I had expected. On the way back I saw a super camera shot. The sun had just set and Blakeney Church stood silhouetted against a flaming sky, all of which was reflected in the flooded marsh, smoothly rippled as a swan glided across. I lifted the camera to find that the film had run out. A few days later I took the children onto Morston Strand to gather cockles for tea. The piles of tangle thrown up onto the fields were enormous, further evidence for how big a tide it had been. Looking towards Wells, we saw what looked and sounded like a wasps' nest of RAF helicopters bringing sandbags to fill the breaches in the Beach Road bank there. Later they did the same at Cley.

The 78 event tends to get forgotten but in scale it was just as severe as that of December 5th 2014 and possibly worse.

17 Graham Walker

This book is an attempt to show the reality of this coast through the prism of my life, but this chapter is an exception. It reflects that reality through the experience of a friend – an experience it is a privilege to share. Graham and I met on our first day at Wells Secondary Modern. We were friends during our four years there and went on to Lynn College, were we lodged together for two more years. We got into considerable mischief at both places. Once, when we were moved on to new lodgings, he turned his shirt back to front, put on a black sweater and I took him round the neighbourhood to introduce him as the new vicar. We were always a bit wild but I have always believed that wildness in youth foretells character in later life. While I'm not able to judge the veracity of that in my own case, it was certainly true in his. He went on to be a member of Wells Lifeboat crew and eventually became coxswain and Harbour Master. I'm sure that back then neither of us would have expected to lead the lives we did. But we always kept in touch and I seldom sailed along the coast without calling him at the Lifeboat Station on the radio to let him know what I was doing, even though I would have been mortally embarrassed if I'd had to call him out.

Graham when Coxswain

The winter of 1979 produced some of the worst weather of the 20th century, and on February 15th it reached a climax with sub-zero temperatures and blizzards. Thinking that an event of such severity could be something they might witness only once in their lives, I wanted my children to see and remember it. So, after getting them well rugged, I took them just a half-mile out of the village, but conditions quickly became so bad that I began to doubt we would get back safely. I took a few photographs and we battled our way home. The roads in and out of the village were blocked with huge snowdrifts, and the snow blown by storm force winds reduced visibility to almost nothing. When later I learned that the Wells Lifeboat had been out for eleven hours in those conditions, I couldn't believe it. It was incredible that anyone would have the courage to try to get out of Wells Harbour, or that they would succeed without being turned back end over end. This is the story of those eleven hours. Forty miles east of the Humber estuary on

This is my son Mark standing in the road on the afternoon of that day. We retreated after making half a mile for fear of not being able to get home. At that time Graham and the crew of the Ernest Tom Neathercoat were miles off shore fighting raging seas.

this terrible day, the MV Savinesti, with 28 people aboard, suffered engine failure. She put her anchor out but it was dragging and she was in grave danger of drifting onto Race Bank or Docking Shoal where in such conditions she would almost certainly have been wrecked. Wells lifeboat station was contacted by Yarmouth coastguard, and asked to launch. The much bigger Humber lifeboat had been diverted to another service, and the seas crashing against the doors of Cromer lifeboat station prevented them from launching. Wells lifeboat offered the last chance those people might have. The crew, including Graham, assembled at the boathouse and were waiting to board. The secretary, David Case, recalls saying to the coxswain, David Cox: "David, this isn't fit for an open boat like ours". Realising that the Cromer boat couldn't go, David in his quiet way just said, "We'll have a look". It was decided that each man could choose whether or not to go, but no-one dropped out. The boat was launched and proceeded toward the harbour entrance. David Cox took it very easy, giving everyone the chance to get their oilskins as wind- and water-proof as they could. It had been impossible to see the bar from the boathouse, and the seas when they got there were very heavy. Nevertheless they decided, as they put it, to "have a go". David opened the throttles halfway and headed out of the harbour. Crossing the bar was a hair-raising experience, being hit from all directions by the confused seas. Once clear of the bar, things became marginally easier and they set course for the Race Bank. All the time, the north-east wind was increasing and seas were breaking over them, causing the Ernest Tom to labour, shuddering each time she lifted her head after burying in a large wave and the coxswain had to pull back on the throttles. Suddenly there was a shout from one of the crew as a huge sea curled up on the starboard side. The coxswain quickly eased back further as they were totally engulfed with green sea. The boat reared up and ended on her beam ends (her side) to port, under water halfway up her decks. Lifebelts save lives, but in situations like that they also lift you off your feet at the time you most need them to be firmly planted on the deck. After a head count, thankfully, they continued on their way. The ferocity of the seas hitting them had disabled the radar, the MF radio and the echo-sounder. Once again they were knocked down by a tremendous wave. On her beam ends again, she hung there hesitating, as if wondering whether it would be easier to turn over completely before rolling back onto an even keel. Continuing to increase, the wind was blowing the snow horizontally. Even the bow of the boat became invisible, and the temperature was minus four. The crew, all frozen with cold, were being thrown all over the place. None had ever been subject to such violence at sea before.

VHF transmission was received, telling them that the Savinesti was two-and-a-half miles from the South Race Buoy and that a North Sea ferry, the Norwave, had arrived on the scene. The coxswain had kept them offshore (to the east) of the Savinesti, and when he considered they had come the right distance turned west toward her. Taking this course put the seas on her stern and the drogue had to be deployed[1]. Under normal conditions this would have taken about five minutes, but the crews' hands were frozen, as were the ropes holding the drogue. These were eventually cut and it was put over the stern, the lines played out and secured. The seas were coming at them on the starboard quarter (that is from behind but slightly to the right), and each time they were hit by a sea the rope went as tight as a rod of steel. They had not gone far when a large shadow (described as like a row of houses) loomed ahead, and as they eased down the Savinesti came into view to the north, along with a merchant ship, the Annuity, and the massive outline of the Norwave dodging to the south. By this time the conditions had deteriorated badly. The wind had risen from storm to hurricane force from the north-east, with forty-foot seas breaking over the shoaling sandbanks. In these conditions they stayed on station with the Savinesti for two hours until a relayed signal via Norwave from Yarmouth coastguard told them that the 54ft Humber Lifeboat, the Aran, was almost with them and they were released.

Spectacular seas were now breaking over the sandbanks on a scale that none of them had seen before and would probably never see again. The station record says that the seas were 50-60ft. The Norwave gave them a wind speed of force 11 gusting to hurricane force 12, and the bearing for the south-east Docking buoy. This course meant that the Ernest Tom would be in the most dangerous situation of having a following sea all the way back. If a boat is carried forward at great speed by a following sea, it can easily be rolled over. In the event it became impossible to steer the given course with such huge waves. The best they could manage was a south-westerly track. The drogue was whining and cracking, going slack and then all the water squeezed out of it as it came bar-tight. If it had broken they would have been turned over. Two of the crew were told to face aft and warn of any potentially overwhelming seas. This return was probably the worst part of the service. The wind was throwing snow in their faces at 80 mph, and with the air at minus four all the crew were frozen. Graham said he had no feeling at all from the waist down, or in his hands and arms. So cold were they that the seas breaking over them felt warm. A hot drink or a little food would have made a difference. They each had two squares of chocolate which, with frozen hands, were devoured foil and all. At Race Bank they witnessed what can only be described as a maelstrom. The wind combined with the tide-rip over the shallow water created a raging tumult, seas crashing into each other like battling titans and rising high into the sky.

Vast amounts of the North Sea rose so high that they could see clear under it before it crashed back into the turmoil. Running with the sea and wind behind them, the atmosphere was very subdued. Very little was said. All must have been thinking that if they survived it would be a miracle. After two hours the motion of the boat changed. The seas became increasingly confused, and with no echo-sounder and zero visibility it was difficult to be certain of their position, but it was thought they could be among the shallow ridges off Holkham Bay.

After some discussion between David Cox and Tony Jordan, the second coxswain, it was decided to head out to the north to get clear. For the first time since their departure they began to get a weak VHF carrier signal, which they thought might be from the coastguards. They sent a reply but got no answer. With their damaged aerial they might have been heard but were unable to pick up the reply. If this was the case, then there could have been auxiliaries posted along the coast looking for some sign of them. It was decided to fire one white parachute flare. These could get up to a thousand feet clear of the scud and bad visibility, but to their despair there was no response, no reply, nothing.

Things were now very serious. In failing light, with the wind still hurricane force and in shallow water, the steeper seas were more likely to overwhelm them. This, combined with a lee shore an unknown distance away, threatened a very quick end to their suffering. Then at this lowest point, as if by divine intervention, it cleared – not a lot, but enough for Graham to see a light dead ahead, faint but then another. A parachute flare was fired and then after a bit the VHF burst out: "Wells Lifeboat – Wells Lifeboat – Scolt Two – Scolt Two." Boy Court, the mechanic, said: "Who the hell is Scolt Two?" It was Richard Sutherland, a Brancaster fisherman in a Land Rover on Brancaster Beach road. He quickly gave them their position as one mile north-east of Brancaster wreck buoy and heading for certain disaster. Instantly the coxswain turned the Ernest Tom to port and a heading of due east. At last they were heading for Wells, but it got no easier. The compass was unstable, spinning wildly and unwilling to settle on any definite point, and an easterly course meant that every large wave

The 'Ernest Tom' as she was at that time.

threatened to thrust the bow shoreward; so the coxswain had to turn her to face each one. The seven miles to the fairway buoy took them another two hours. Nearing it, their troubles were far from over. They still had to get over the bar, and the seas by this time were more ferocious than when they had left eleven hours earlier. It was impossible for them to see the shore or any buoys. Once more the radio sprang into life. "Wells Lifeboat – Wells Lifeboat – This is Strandline – This is Strandline – Do you receive?" It was John Ward who, knowing how difficult their re-entry would be, had brought his boat as far down the channel as he could to give them a point to run into. One mile out, David put the Ernest Tom on a line, and with the drogue set at its fullest extent to stop her from surfing, began the run in. She took the seas well, and although two or three broke over her they gained the shelter of the harbour safely at 21.12. The relief among them was palpable. To return alive against such odds, to be secure once more in the shelter of the harbour they never thought they would reach, was a feeling only they could describe. The tractor to tow them back to the station was unavailable, another casualty of the storm, so they went up to the quay and tied up alongside a coaster.

They were then astounded and deeply touched by how many people had turned out on such a terrible night to welcome them. Graham remembers noticing, as he was more or less carried across the deck of the coaster, seeing bottles of rum and whisky set out on the hatch by people who thought it would put life back into their frozen bodies. As the tears burned in his eyes, so was the whole of that ordeal on his memory.

---

1. Drogue or Sea Anchor = a device like a paracute that is thrown over to act as a brake.

February 15th 1979. Silver medal awarded to Coxswain David Cox in recognition of his courage, determination and seamanship when the lifeboat under his command stood by the Rumanian cargo vessel 'Savinesti' which had broken down and lost both her anchors north of the South Race Buoy in a nort- easterly hurricane, extremely poor visibility due to heavy snow, sub zero temperatures and very rough sea. Coxswain David Cox recalls the following details of this service.

"The weather was heavily overcast with a north easterly gale blowing and it had been snowing. I happened to be coming out of the Wells Health Care Centre at about 10 a.m. when the maroons went up and I immediately went down to the boathouse and got on the phone to Yarmouth Coastguards. They told me that a vessel was in trouble north of the South Race Buoy as she had lost two anchors and could not hold up into the weather, there was fear that she would drift onto the Race Bank where the water was very shallow."

The crews that day comprised.............

David Cox	Coxswain
Tony Jordan	2nd Coxswain
Albert Court	Mechanic
Alan M Cox	Assistant Mechanic
Albert Warner	Crew Member
John R Nudds	Crew Member
Graham Walker	Crew Member
John W Betts	Crew Member

18 The Watch House

In the late 1960s when our children were still small, Beano asked me if I would like to take over from him as caretaker of the Watch House. The Watch House was on lease to the Girl Guide Association, and it was for them that I was to take care. I have done that for the house ever since, though these days it is as chairman of the Watch House Trust. It wasn't a particularly onerous job – a bit of painting, some occasional minor repairs, and I had to ensure they always had gas. From time to time film and TV people would use it, and the money I asked from them went into the gas kitty. I am quite proud that during the 25 years that I acted as their caretaker, the Guides never had to pay for gas. The Guides' use was sporadic, so there were weeks free when we could use it ourselves. The Watch House became our summer home for many years while the children were small. I'd had a dinghy made to the same design as Beano's, which I painted bright red, and the children named it Ishy Bishy Barny Bee. This was a special time for my family.

Some stays were in high summer; others could be quite late in the year. One October we were there for two weeks, during which there was a big storm. The house was shaking with the impacts of the waves on the beach when I awoke. The view from the lookout revealed little but water. None of the beach was visible as huge waves were breaking over it, and blowing spume filled the space between it and the house. The view from the windows was blurred by condensation and I left it that way, not wanting the children to be alarmed by discovering the house was sitting on such a small island. It was quite a surreal feeling to be so cosy around the fire, having breakfast trapped in the midst of such turmoil.

One summer, my friend Martin Ryle had been ill, and he and his wife Rowena were staying at their cottage in Cley. I knew he hadn't been out on the water for a couple of years, so I was determined to get him out there if I could. Before taking the family across I went to see him. When I arrived, Rowena said he'd just popped across the road to see the Dean of St Paul's. I thought: is this really Cley-next-the Sea? While I sat talking to Rowena, a woman came in who had just climbed Mount Everest. She was still there when Martin came back with the Dean. Not for the first time I wondered how a small wader like me could flap his wings hard enough to stay aloft with such high fliers.

When they left I had a long and enjoyable talk with Martin. He was keen to come if I could collect him. So, weather permitting, we made a date for later that week. Although the children always got unbroken stays, I still had to come back sometimes to work. On the third day I returned to work in my studio during the morning, before going to see Martin. He told me there had been a big crime. Cley Stores had been robbed. The thieves had tried to make their getaway in Richard Newton's van but had only gone a short distance before it ran out of petrol. They then switched to another one and made their escape. When I got back out to the Watch House, Richard and his wife Annalise were there, but when I asked him about it he took a step back. That was the first he knew of it. They had left to come out to us without even noticing that the van had gone.

I took him down to the Lifeboat House at the end of the Point so he could ring the police. Apparently the thieves had used his drill to break into the Post Office. I wondered if that made him an accessory. Later he and I netted Cley channel and splashed for Butts[1]. We saw a few but we had no luck. I wasn't too disappointed about that, as they taste bloody awful. In the evening my son Toby and I went to gather firewood. As we walked along the beach the sun was going down and golden backlit flecks of foam were chasing each other up the beach. We found an old pallet and some rope, and made a sled to drag our haul of wood.

Odd how such small, precious moments stick in your mind. I got up early next day and had a very cold run back across the mud in bare feet. I worked in the studio again and needed to get my work finished as I was taking Martin over at 11.am. It turned into the most beautiful day. As we motored over, the sun was hot and the wind non-existent. Rowena was so happy to have Martin back on the water again.

They enjoyed it so much that we did the same the next day, when we had a little longer on the tide. I came to know Martin when I was painting the 3D space pictures (see page 97) and Rowena shared an exhibition with me at the Assembly House in Norwich.

---

1. Butts= Harbour flat fish able to tolerate brackish water.

Most of us will have met people who were superlatively brilliant in one field but unable to find their way out of a paper bag in any other. Martin, who was Astronomer Royal from 1972 to 1982, had a particular type of genius – of which more in the concluding chapters – of academic brilliance and artisan skills in equal measure. He could visualise something and then design and build it. The Mullard Astronomy site in Cambridge, of which Martin was the founding director, covers a big area, and to get around it they used old mopeds. One of the routes crossed a disused railway track, which bisected the site. One day out of curiosity, Martin checked it with a compass. It turned out to run precisely north to south. This gave him the idea for the aperture synthesis array that went on to discover the first pulsar[1] and became the foundation for the Mullard Radio Astronomy Observatory. Martin conceived this telescope, oversaw its construction and built the computer to interpret its results.

He showed me round the site, and that computer filled a complete building. But his genius allowed him to make furniture and build boats. He was also special in a way that is common to every one of the best people I have been fortunate enough to know. He treated everyone the same. His common touch, an oxymoron if ever there was one – was typified for me on two occasions. The signature signal for a pulsar is a regular one-second burst of radio waves, and nothing as brief as that had ever been detected before. One of the obvious first possibilities for such a signal was intelligent life, hence its being logged as LGM1 (Little Green Men 1). On the evening of that discovery Martin, bursting to tell someone, rang me. On the day he learned he had been awarded the Nobel Prize for Physics, he and Rowena had a house full of celebrating university friends, yet he still found the time to spend half an hour talking to me on the phone about it. Martin came to the Watch House again the next year, and many other friends would join us there during the years of our use. I was caretaker for more than 25 years until structural problems ended the Guides use.

1.= A highly magnetized, rotating neutron star that emits a beam of electromagnetic radiation.

The House

The Watch House is situated on Blakeney Point atop a lateral ridge roughly halfway along the shingle bank between Cley Beach and the end of the Point. There is some uncertainty about when it was built. It is thought to date from the early 1830s, but that presents a bit of a puzzle because it has cavity walls, which didn't come into general use until very much later. It was the cavity walls that led to the Guides finally letting it go. A routine inspection in 1992 showed that the front wall was collapsing outward. The primitive metal ties had rusted away, and the two walls were no longer held together. The Watch House had been much more seriously damaged in 1953, and at that time the Guides had been able to raise the money to repair it. But overcoming the ravages of the '53 storm proved easier than overcoming modern bureaucracy. This time they failed, so the house was closed and cordoned off. The future looked bleak. The National Trust made it clear they did not have the funds to repair it. While they appreciated its value as a feature in the landscape, if a solution wasn't found they would pull it down.

19 Infinity and Beyond

When my eldest son Mark was five, he was given a box of paints for Christmas. To show him how to use them, I painted some local scenes on the backs of some of the Christmas cards. Judy, who isn't easy to impress (lifting cars full of people didn't do it), thought they were good, which encouraged me to do some more. I painted boats and ships and flowers, and it proved an excellent antidote to the stresses of tight driving schedules. Between the first moon landing in 1969 and the success of the Mariner 9 mission to Mars in 1971, my enthusiasm for astronomy and science fiction caused me to think about how some of the things in space might look. Mariner 9 sent back some fuzzy black-and-white images of the Tithonius Lacus canyon on Mars, and from these I imagined how the Martian surface might look in colour. I painted nebulae, the Earth from the moon and spacecraft travelling through the solar system powered by sun sails. I thought there might be a market for such work as covers for sci-fi books. Having photographed my paintings, I got a surprise the first time I put one of the slides into the viewer. The light shining through from behind made the stars shine, and the black of space became infinite. It was a 'eureka' moment. If there was a way to recreate that effect with a full size painting, I really would have something nobody had seen before. But how to do it?

My first idea was to paint on a transparent screen and put a bank of fluorescent tubes behind it. But then one evening at a dance I noticed how white shirts and blouses shone in ultra violet light, and realised that the answer might lie there. I bought a large ultra-violet bulb and began experimenting. I knew they put something into washing powder to reflect UV to make shirts, as they said, 'whiter than white'. I tried boiling it to extract whatever it was that did it, but without success. I even painted a picture with Persil. Not many artists will have done that. Weird as it sounds, it sort of worked, producing little sparkles of light under the UV bulb. But I was never going to be able to paint with it, so, passing up the only chance I'll probably ever have to be whiter than white, I moved on. I had been thinking about fluorescent paint for some time. Its Dayglo colours had put me off, but after all the other failed attempts it seemed worth a try. To my delight the colours worked pretty much as normal ones do. As soon as two or more were

mixed together the vividness disappeared. The first small attempts worked so well that I could hardly contain myself. Under a UV strip, the stars shone brightly and you could reach into the black to your armpit and still not touch them.

I then began work on much bigger paintings. I found some 6ft x 4ft board with a surface I could use, exchanged the normal strip light in the studio for a UV one and I was off. Wearing a beanie hat to keep the flickering light out of my eyes, I worked on the floor. To begin with it was a difficult colour balance, as the way the colours appeared in white light could dramatically change when the UV strip was switched on. Once I got the measure of that, I started to get results. One of the other problems was getting realistic star fields. No matter how I painted them, eyes shut, left-handed, on my back, upside down, they always came out with stars too evenly distributed and looking like early black-and-white sci-fi film backdrops. I then realised something important. We think and act in an ordered way, and expect order even where there is none. The star fields of our galaxy epitomise the asymmetry of our lives as well as the universe. The clouds of the Milky Way, stars clustered together, tight bunches like the Pleiades, loose strings like the Great Bear - nowhere are they evenly spread.

Amateur flower painters always depict each flower facing the viewer, complete and posing for its portrait, and the result is wallpaper. That is not how the world is. In nature, flowers like everything else are haphazard, nodding every which way and hiding one behind another. This was a lesson that had implications for a great deal more than just painting, but at that moment I had to find a way to put randomness into star painting. The solution was to lay the black-painted board on the lawn, take my stars upstairs and chuck them out of the window. There were a number of ways to do this. For the fine and very distant stars I used a toothbrush, scrubbing it with my fingernail to flick a spray of paint out into the air. For the mainstream stars I would spit it out (any neighbours looking must have thought I was vomiting out of the window) or flick it off my fingers. I was then able to paint the nearer, brighter stars and constellations by hand. Once the paint left my mouth or the toothbrush, its trajectory was determined by its own aerodynamics. During its fall, chaos intervened, and as it fell onto the painting surface a more natural universe was created. This was an important breakthrough because not only did the star fields look right, but I'd also shortened my name from Godfrey to God, a maker of worlds.

I then had to work out how I would display them. The answer was to put them in strong heavy frames with a UV strip light built into the top. This worked well, but only in low artificial light. Extending it further out from the frame helped, but I knew this was an insoluble problem. UV just could not compete with white light. So the display options would be confined to places where I could have some control over the ambient light.

While sitting having a drink before a concert at the Norwich Theatre Royal one evening, I noticed they had display bays set back from the main corridor which needed their own lighting. I could see straight away that they would be perfect. I checked to see if there were convenient power sockets and arranged to have an exhibition. I took four of the 4ft x 6 ft works, including a large one of Mars with its moons, and they all fitted perfectly. As I stood looking at them and feeling very pleased, I heard women's voices approaching. This was my first exhibition of any kind and I was very keen to know what people would make of it, so I hid where I could watch their reaction. They turned out to be the cleaning ladies and duly stopped in front of the Mars painting. "What do you think that is?" one said, pointing with a scrubbing brush. "I dunno," said the other. "Looks like a bleedin' orange to me!" My first audience reaction. It could only get better.

At this time the first samples of moon rock were touring British universities. Professor Peter Brimblecombe, professor of atmospheric chemistry at the University of East Anglia, invited me to illustrate the UEA lecture theatre when the samples came to Norwich. I decided to paint a moonscape especially for the event, basing it on the concept used in bird magazines where a coloured picture is accompanied by a numbered black and white drawing to help you identify each species. I hoped this would give a little reference to the lecturer and it did. As he put each sample slide onto the screen, the professor used his wand to point to the painting and say something like, "These low flat hills have been worn down by meteorite rain", or "This is a sample of impact ejecta, a piece of which you can see here", and (moving the wand) "here is the crater from which it came".

I sat at the back with a head as big as bucket. I sold only one or two space paintings. Although the equipment and framing made them quite expensive, I don't think cost was the problem. My conclusion at the time was that only a relatively small proportion of the population were interested in space, and among those an even smaller proportion were interested in paintings. But it was never a waste. I had done what I set out to do. I had recreated the 3D effect I had seen through the slide viewer, and I had done it far better than I had ever hoped. It also gave me the confidence to paint to sell, and that is the only reason I give here for straying so far from the coast.

I used to get a red pen through my sums at school, not because they were incorrect but because they were untidy and I think that's where it starts. We seem to need order. When I was on Blakeney Parish Council, the Church Council came to us with a plan to fell a mature beechwood to make more room for burials. We were horrified, as there was a suitable area empty on the north side of the church into which the 18th-century headstones on the south side of the church could be moved. The old stones were like an old man's teeth, leaning drunkenly and with irregular gaps between them and in not very straight lines. But they had that unique attractiveness that only comes from being blown around by the winds of time and it seemed important to carry that round to the north side too.

South side with stones removed

So I took photos and drew a plan of the original layout. A local firm was brought in to do the work and I met the foreman to explain what we wanted. Giving him my plan and the photos, I left them to it. When I went back later I found that they had used almost all the stones, erecting them all perfectly perpendicular and equidistant, and in one very straight line. "We're not going to have enough," the foreman said. "We'll only manage another half row." I asked why they hadn't followed the plan. "We thought you were joking," he said, "wanting us to put them in crooked".

North side as it looks now

While nature creates many regular patterns – snowflakes, crystals, basalt columns, etc – the universe we live in is asymmetrical. All of its matter occurs in clumps. The night sky is perhaps the best example, but there are countless others. Randomly generated numbers consistently throw up close sequences, lottery numbers often throw up three numbers in sequence. Cancer clusters are another. A while ago, three people in the same row of houses in our village died over a short space of time from brain tumours. There was the usual concern about electricity wires, but there was no connection. There had been no cases before and there have been none since. It was just clumping. This may also be the explanation for why three buses turn up at once, and why bad luck never comes alone. Whatever, we are conditioned to expect order where there is none, a lesson I believe most artists come to learn.

20 An Abrupt Change of Course

My haulage contract with the BU was for a same-day service. Even the mail was included. I would collect from four or five different departments around the Leicester factory, then drive to Norwich, sometimes via Northampton, to deliver up to five tons of materials and machinery to as many as twelve shoe businesses around the city. If traffic was heavy on the A47, or if there were roadworks, I could often end up cutting it fine. If I had a furniture removal scheduled for the next day, the last thing I wanted was to end up with a heavy undelivered machine in the back.

This began to put quite a strain on me. It only needed a major diversion or a minor mechanical problem to put me in a muddle. I had a one-ton transit van as back-up, but the amount I was carrying by then would have filled it many times over. On the day I decided to pack it in, I had been delayed by traffic, and roadworks had sent me on a long detour which meant I had to approach Norwich on the Fakenham road. Ahead of me was a slow-moving truck carrying enormous blocks of stone. There were several opportunities to get past it, but each time I tried I was thwarted by a cyclist who was slipstreaming it, swinging back and forth out into the road in front of me. This went on for a couple of miles, and my frustration was building. Eventually we stopped at traffic lights. I jumped out, went over to him and told him to stop it. We set off again but at the first opportunity to overtake he swung out again. I blew my horn and he stuck two fingers up. This blew the plug off the volcano and everything turned red. By the time we came to the Norwich ring road roundabout I was choking on my own smoke. The traffic stopped, I leapt out, ran across the road and punched him hard in the side. I remember he had a tight leather jacket on, and it was like hitting a drum. He flew off his bike into the road, landed on his back and began skittering away from me on his backside. I followed him to the kerb with his bike, and as he sat there I put it over his head and pushed it down as firmly as I could, pinning his arms to his sides. As I walked back I noticed that all the traffic on the roundabout had stopped, and everyone was looking either at me or at him sitting there imprisoned by his bicycle. That was the moment I decided to stop driving for a living.

After the Theatre Royal show I'd had one other exhibition at the Norwich Assembly House. This had been moderately successful, and it had encouraged me to think that I could make a living as a painter. Looking back now I can see that my modest ability at that time really didn't justify such a move, especially with three small children. But, perhaps still thinking I was God, I held my nose and went for it. In those days the Church Rooms on the quayside at Blakeney were the village community centre, and it was my plan to have one or maybe two exhibitions there each year. I could always fall back on bait-digging if it didn't bring in enough. But when I asked about it I was told it was booked up with regular exhibitors for at least two years ahead. To rub salt in the wound I then learned that none of these exhibitors lived in Blakeney. In fact most of them didn't even live in Norfolk. I was furious that the village community centre could be used in this way. But I had my heart set on painting; so I looked for another way. My last haulage lorry had a transparent fibreglass roof that let in light, and had more than enough space to hang paintings. So I thought I'll use that. I can park it on the Carnser by the sea bank and it'll be perfect. I took it down to Richard Newton at Cley, and we set about converting it. We panelled out the interior and he made a set of steps – the ones I still use today – to fit on the back, and it was done. I drove it down onto the Carnser and opened the doors. People came in and have done so ever since. But sadly that wasn't quite the end of it.

The Carnser had been used for trading of all kinds for centuries, but at that time Blakeney Parish Council had few indigenous people on it; so there was no support for me, let alone any understanding of community and village history. So they immediately tried to remove me. The Carnser was a free car park and there were others using it for business, including an ice-cream van from another part of Norfolk, but they weren't having me.

The Parish Council had no rules or policies relating to the area at that time, so they had no clear reason for removing me other than that they just didn't want me there. Eventually they brought in North Norfolk District Council, but as luck would have it each time their enforcement officer came out I was at sea with fishing parties. I told Judy to warn him what might happen should he come along when I was there – particularly if he was riding a bike – but he never did. It went on for a year or two, but eventually the parish council got more local people on it, the area became regulated and three trading sites were designated. NNDC continued to insist that the site did not have planning permission, so the possibility of enforcement officers ending up in the quay remained. Eventually I had to put the case to the district council's planning sub-committee, arguing that with property prices off the scale for most locals, the trading sites on the Carnser offered an opportunity for them to get a start in business. This swung the day, although sadly today equality legislation prevents the parish council from keeping them exclusively for locals.

For the first few years I was only able to make a living from painting in the summer, and went back to bait-digging during the winter. It was at this time that I worked on the Point with Beano. If I had to put my finger on where in my life I have been most fortunate – other than meeting my wife – I would have to say that it is in the people I have known and had as friends, people whose opinions I could trust and who had the faith in me that I may not have had in myself. People of experience and wisdom who were there at the right moment. At this time it was Margaret Spurrell, who became my friend at more or less the same time I began to paint. She had been friends with the writer Henry Williamson. As a girl she knew Henry Rider Haggard and was a lifelong friend of his daughter Lilias. She knew Edward Seago and Jack Harrison, the bird painter, who was still alive then and who I was lucky enough to meet a few times. Jack didn't suffer fools, so his support, along with Margaret's, helped to convince me that I had a future as a painter. One winter I injured my back and was unable to dig bait. Margaret had been insisting for some time that I could sell my work through the London West End stores, and kept on at me to make appointments with the buyers. I managed to set up a day of appointments in late December with Harrods, Selfridges, Heal's and Libertys. I came out of Oxford Street tube station early, and before going to get breakfast I went into Libertys and asked if I might leave my portfolio there until my appointment. The girl said that the buyer was already in and she could call him. She did and he appeared immediately. He quickly looked through my folder and said, "Would you like to have an exhibition?" I was speechless. That wasn't at all what I'd expected him to say. They'd had a cancellation for an exhibition in February, and he wanted me to fill it. He said I would need a minimum of seventy paintings. I only had fifteen in my portfolio, so saying yes was quite a commitment. One of the girls rang the other stores and cancelled the rest of my appointments. I then ran back to the tube and came home. I drove straight from the station to Margaret with the news. She was overjoyed, although she said it was no less than she had expected. She was custodian of Lilias's house, which sits high up on the 'Downs' overlooking Blakeney Harbour, and she let me turn a small bedroom which had the most splendid view on the entire Norfolk coast into a studio. I spent the remainder of that day moving all my gear in so that I would be ready to start the next morning. Buoyed by such an opportunity I completed all seventy paintings in time. The exhibition was a success, and I had to paint several more as it proceeded. It was an important milestone for me. For the first time, I was fully professional, painting throughout the year rather just through the summer. This made a big difference to the quality of my work. I exhibited regularly with Liberty over a period of ten years, including two more one-man shows, and this carried me into the time when people began coming up to Norfolk in the winter, which allowed me to sell all year round.

I owe Margaret a lot. She was as dear to me as my mother, and although there were many years between us we became very close. When she became frail at the end of her life, I became her carer, sleeping at her house and helping her with the things she had begun to find difficult. To have had such an intimate and privileged relationship with her was one of the most special gifts I have had in my life.

21 The 1987 Hurricane

I was due to get up quite early that day to take my son to Scotland but was woken at 2.am, by the wind. In the house where we lived in Blakeney at that time, there was a distinct change in tone when the wind got above a certain speed. It turned from a hissing to a roar, and that morning it was roaring. By 5.am when the alarm went off it was howling. I let our little terrier Boots out for a pee and he vanished for about 20 minutes. So hard was it blowing I started to worry that he'd been swept away. I was concerned for my studio, which at that time was a caravan on the Bayfield estate, and decided I had better go and check it. I found the roads full of debris. The Langham to Holt stretch, which was at right angles to the southerly wind, was full of soil blown off the fields, and this after some of the heaviest rain for years. The car was being so thrown about that I felt sure I would have to cancel the trip to Scotland.

My son arrived shortly after I got back at 6.am, delayed by not being able to find a way out of Letheringsett for fallen trees. In the end he got through by moving one himself. It was difficult to decide what to do. The radio was giving out hurricane warnings and advising people to stay indoors and not to travel – the sort of news that usually just makes me want to get out and experience it. Such very high winds don't usually last very long, so I came up with a compromise. I was worried about Ebbtide, my four-berth cruiser which was then moored in the Pit, and really wanted to go and check her out, so I said I would go and do that first, then decide what to do about the drive to Scotland.

My journey out in the half-light was hard, like having a bully constantly pushing me in the back, making me slither and stumble across the marsh at a half-run. When I got to the Pit it dawned on me that even if I did row out to Ebbtide I probably wouldn't be able to row back against such a wind. Then, as if in response to my thoughts, all the wind in the world began to blow. I climbed inside a heavy dinghy and crouched down with just my head above the gunwale. From here I watched a sight unfold that was more extreme than anything I had ever seen. Having such a long clear run at it, the wind had no bounds. As its power increased, so the heavy boat I was in began slowly nudging sideways. The surface of the Pit began to be torn off and lifted into the air, and like a sandstorm was being carried away up toward the Point. The boats disappeared in a moving screen of water. It was as if the Pit were a boiling cauldron, the spray coming off it like steam up to four feet above the surface. Then, just when it seemed it had reached its peak, it began to rain hard and everything disappeared. The maelstrom only lasted for about ten minutes, then the wind eased. Grabbing my chance, I righted my dinghy, which was upside down, and rowed out as fast as I could. Ebbtide was secured and well battened down. All I had to do was pump out some water. I then had to wait in a world of flying water and a banshee screaming of rigging until the wind eased again. When it did, I rowed furiously for the shore. A second blast of wind on the way back over the marsh pinned me down for a while but it did seem overall to be easing.

The Pit is a large area of open water between Blakeney Point and the saltmarshes which remains deep enough for many moored boats to float at low water and so is the principial mooring area for larger boats.

We decided we would go to Scotland, and set off soon after I returned. Fallen trees and branches delayed us for the first part of the journey, but we were soon out of the hurricane's path and on our way. Its effects didn't seem to extend much further north than Sleaford

It's an ill wind that blows no good, they say, and certainly this was a very ill wind. But a few years later, when I rebuilt the old Summer House on the Bayfield estate to use as a studio, all the timber came from oaks and chestnut trees blown down that day. Trees on the outside of woods develop a greater resistance to wind than those inside that are sheltered. The south is not a direction from which we get strong winds – south-west yes, but not due south – so I wonder if the huge number of trees that were blown down was greater because they had less resistance to winds from that direction.

22 Rewritten Scripts

I have been mysteriously rescued from near disaster so many times that the philosophy of my life has become shaped by it. I suspect that most people when taking on, or facing, life's challenges do so with confidence or trepidation based on past sucesses or failures. So many times I have been pulled from the mire by this mysterious hand, that I have come to rely on it, and so far it has always been there.

Dredging the Cut

At the time Margaret Spurrell was becoming frail, I was chairman of a committee set up by Blakeney Parish Council to dredge the channel. We had worked hard for two years raising well over £30,000 (no mean feat in the 1980s). The dragline was coming, the National Trust had given us permission to put the spoil on the adjoining marsh and we seemed clear to go. But at that moment I got a letter from the Board of Trade asking if I was aware that a royalty of 10p was payable for every cubic metre of material we took out. This was a hammer blow. To have spent so much time and effort raising money, and then have to give a large chunk of it to the government, was worse than infuriating. It would ruin the project and make us very unpopular with those who had made donations. By this time I had been caring for Margaret for several weeks. Her godson was coming to see her and asked to meet me to discuss her future. He came, we met and chatted, and I discovered that he was Under Secretary of State for Transport. He said he was concerned that Margaret's care had just devolved on to me without my appearing to have had much say in it, and that he felt he should repay me in some way. I assured him that there was absolutely no imbalance in the arrangement and he needn't think any more about it. Then I remembered the levy.

I suggested a walk and took him down to the stretch of channel we were hoping to dredge. "While you owe me nothing for what I do for Margaret," I said, "the people who have worked so hard to raise the money for this would be eternally grateful if you could get us round this obstacle."A short time later I got a letter inviting me to Whitehall. Bring anything you can to show what you are doing, it said. I organised the trip to coincide with a delivery of paintings to Liberty, which I got done first. Then I went to learn our fate. I was shown to the office of a Mr Purkis, who seemed very friendly, and we sat and talked about the dredging plans. I showed him some maps and aerial photographs. Then, after a bit, he offered to get me a cup of coffee. He disappeared for a few minutes then came back and said, "I've had a word with my boss, and he says if you give us twenty quid that'll do." Having always had to work hard for every penny, I looked the gift horse in the mouth and said, "If you can make it as little as twenty quid, couldn't you just make it nothing?" "No," he replied, "the £20 is for a licence. You are bound to have people complaining when you move their moorings. When they do, just give them this address and we'll deal with it". Once again I came home from London cock-a-hoop. It was such a relief that we could now get full value for the money we had raised.

Village Design Statement

While serving on the Norfolk Coast Project I met David Vose, who worked for what was then called the Countryside Commission. At that time Wiveton had just been through a contentious planning wrangle. At the district council's planning sub-committee meeting, it was clear that the outcome was pre-ordained. The process was running on rails entirely determined by planning policy and with little acknowledgement of the views of the people affected. David and I discussed this, and agreed that there ought to be a way for people in small towns and villages to identify the things they valued most in their communities, and to have them included in the planning process, preferably as planning guidance. A year later we met again and he offered Wiveton the chance to be a pilot for just such a scheme, to be called a Village Design Statement.

It was a chance the people of Wiveton were not going to waste. A group quickly came together and, with match funding from the Countryside Commission, set about evaluating the village. We took photographs and drew maps.

The district council's conservation officer came and walked the village with us, looking at all the buildings.

In the final booklet we described the views out of and into the village, highlighted elements of the village's history, the character of its buildings, the absence of intrusive street furniture and the quality of the environment, for people and for wildlife. The unusual open form of the village, with water meadows and large gardens, linked by hedges, bits of woodland and ditches, creates a wonderful mosaic of habitats used by a great variety of wildlife. So considerable emphasis was placed on this, and how the wellfare of wildlife is inextricably tied in with the development of the built environment.

It was a major task but after several months of enthusiastic work, we had all we needed for a really outstanding document. But we knew that it could miss the mark if we did not present it well. Most planning policy documents are dry and unimaginatively designed, as dull as the bureaucracy that has produced them. But our booklet had to be different it had to influence the elected members as well as the officers. It needed to have visual impact - and that could only be achieved with really good design.

We needed the best graphic designer we could get, but we didn't know any. With all the grant money set aside for the printing, we couldn't afford one anyway. At that time my daughter and her husband were running the Carpenter's Arms pub in Wighton, and one evening she introduced me to John Mitchell.

With some people you just hit the ground running. I liked him instantly. We soon discovered common interests and we talked as if we had known each other all our lives.

Inevitably Wiveton's VDS came up and I told him of our problem. "That sounds like a really good thing to do," he said. " Would you like me to design it for you?" I couldn't believe it. I didn't know he was a graphic designer, let alone, as it later transpired, one of the best.

His only condition was that I went along and did it with him, and this turned out to be a great stroke of luck for me. As the booklet took shape so I began to learn the rudiments of graphic design. "The rules are just the same for this as for what you do" he said. So once again the person I needed appeared out of the sun right on cue.

An old man with Chicken Wire

I had run out of paint and gone in a hurry to get some from the Platten & Anthony hardware store in Wells, where my cycling companion Nigel Starman works. Almost running into the shop, I found my way to the paint blocked by a very old man clutching a roll of chicken wire. Pushing past him I said, to lighten my rudeness, "Just enough to go round the wife." His eyes widened. I glanced up at Nigel and saw his eyes go down. "Oh bugger," I thought. "I've said the wrong thing." Getting my paint, I hurried round the other end of the shelves to escape but bumped into the old man again, still clutching the wire and still blocking my way. "Yew know me, daunt ya," he said. "Yes ol' partner," I replied. "Course I do." Then I dashed to the counter to get out as quickly as I could.

That evening Nigel rang and said, "Saved again, Godders. As your friend Mike says , 'God keeps rewriting the script for you."That old man with the chicken wire, to whom you said 'Just enough to go round the wife', lives just up the road and has been coming in every day for a couple of weeks. His wife recently died and he's distressed and lonely. He's made a small flowerbed at the top of his garden and planted out his wife's name in bedding plants, but the rabbits keep eating them and he wanted the wire to go round her name."

23 Small World, Wide Horizons

Ebbtide

In 1984 I realised a dream and bought a four-berth cruiser. She was a 24ft, Maurice Griffiths-designed Eventide called Ebbtide. I sailed her to Boston a few times, and an aborted trip to Holland left me in Burgh Castle marina for the best part of one summer, but mostly I just sailed the north Norfolk coast on or between tides. While she was imprisoned by northerly winds at Burgh Castle, however, I made an interesting discovery. Sailing out of Blakeney in a small vessel has the ever-present danger of bad weather precluding a return – particularly between tides, because Blakeney bar is impassable in strong onshore winds. But sailing for me was such a special thing. Once over the bar, it felt as if the wind was blowing through me, leaving my mind free of everyday irritations. But there was always a small knot of anxiety just below the surface. If the wind increased, as north-easterly summer breezes often do, that knot would grow and the thought of a long run to Yarmouth or into the Wash would start to erode the pleasure. If conditions did become difficult, there was always great satisfaction in getting safely back onto the mooring without mishap. But that of course was afterwards.

One day when light to moderate north-easterly winds were forecast, it suddenly occurred to me that it would be a perfect moment to sail up the river Yare from Burgh Castle to Reedham Ferry. I thought that Roger Brett, a friend since childhood from Cley, would enjoy such a trip and invited him to come along. We set off with Boots, our Jack Russell, bouncing eagerly along too. It was a lovely day, perfect for such a sail, and I was looking forward to a cruise that didn't involve the worry knot. We glided up the Yare at a fast clip. On some stretches where the path was close to the bank, I let Boots off so he could run alongside. He loved that and, intelligent little dog that he was, he seemed to understand that there was no time to stop for smells.

It was every bit as perfect as I had hoped it would be, and yet it wasn't. It was fun to be clipping along at such a pace and anticipating every new view as we rounded the bends, but the element I thought I could happily do without, the risk of unexpected consequences, wasn't there. How little we know ourselves! The knot of anxiety, of being alone at sea, out of sight

Roger with Boots on the lookout

of land, of big waves, constant sail adjustments and the infinitely varied challenges of wind and tide, was all gone. It was tame, and ultimately it would have become boring. I knew then why I wanted to sail at sea. I needed the risk.

The second year with Ebbtide, I decided I would have a few days up the creeks behind Wells East Hills. I waited for suitable tides and good weather, which were forecast soon to coincide. I got my painting stuff and other supplies together, and took them out to Ebbtide on the evening before. But when the day came it looked less certain that I could go. I'd looked at the sea at Cley beach, where a north-easterly breeze had kicked up a bit of a chop. I resolved to go anyway, and decide what to do when I got to the harbour entrance. With the wind against the tide, it was a little bumpy getting over the bar. I was fortunate that I had pushed out early and wasn't in the worst of it for long. It remained lively when I was clear of the bar but I decided to press on. With a following wind and sea, I fairly ripped along. Blakeney Bar to Wells Bar in one hour twenty minutes against the tide. The wind increased slowly during the trip and the sea looked quite hostile astern, steep with white caps. Little Ishy, being towed behind, looked like a surfboard as it skittered along. It seemed quite incongruous for such a small boat to be out in such waves. As I neared Wells outer buoys it looked much rougher, with a lot of white water across the entrance, but with a firm wind behind me I didn't see any reason to falter. As we surfed in between the outer buoys I suddenly heard a much louder hissing astern, and turned to see Ishy perched on the crest of a wave about six feet above my head. I turned quickly forward again and pretended I hadn't seen.

We got in without mishap and were met by the Wells inshore lifeboat. I'm not sure whether they had come out especially to meet me or were just out for a training run. I knew the helmsman and we had the usual lewd banter – grand to be so welcomed. It was more or less high water, so I was able to motor-sail up past the quay and then back out through Sluice Creek. I wound my way out until we were as close to East Hills as Ebbtide could get with room to turn, and dropped anchor in a spot where I knew she would float at low water. I hate sleeping on the sosh. It took three hours and one minute from casting off to dropping anchor. Not bad. I tidied everything up and then, with the tide under me, rowed the dinghy back up to the quay. I left my oars with a friend at the hardware shop and managed to hitch two lifts that got me home.

In the evening Judy took me back with the rest of my gear. I wanted to take Boots but he got himself wet, and I thought a cold night on board would not be good for him. In any case, he always crawled into my sleeping bag, and I didn't want to sleep with a wet dog. I awoke at 8 am having slept very well, and stuck my head out of the hatch to find it was a beautiful day. Resisting the urge to jump ashore and run about, I made a cup of tea and turned in for another half-hour. Just feeling so warm and comfortable in such a wild place was good enough. I had intended to lie in longer but it was such a glorious morning that I couldn't miss it. I cooked some bacon and eggs, with brown baps and marmalade to follow, then set off for East Hills. I used much of my film on the way out, so once there I settled down to sketch. In such places I soon become aware that I am without people but not alone. There are too many other creatures sharing the sky and marsh for that, but there wasn't another human for miles. This is what makes it such a privileged experience. Wells people do come out here, but not many and not often. On such a vivid day it wasn't hard to see why the place has always had such a hold on me. It isn't an ancient landscape with long human associations. The pines are barely two generations old and the arc of dunes during my time have added at least a quarter to their volume. It holds the remains of someone I once loved a lifetime ago, but it had its hold on me long before then. It is where I am most at home, and if my ghost is to walk anywhere it will be here. The reason why this should be so isn't at all clear. It could be the view. With the huge sky, the autumnal hues of the marsh and soft ochres of the waving grasses, it might just be that it is beautiful. But why do I feel this so much more than other people? I'll come to that later.

I did a couple of sketches and painted a view of Wells with foreground pines, but started back for Ebbtide when I noticed that the tide was making. I had only been back aboard about five minutes when the tide arrived and, shortly after that, intent on proving me wrong, a man and woman in a small dinghy. After an hour of scudding clouds the sun came out to stay, and it became warm. The wind was quite fresh but as Ebbtide was lying directly into the wind I had shelter from it in the cockpit. So, for a while until the work ethic briefly surfaced, I sunbathed. The painting I did was of Wells looking back down Sluice Creek. Later the couple drifted back past on the ebb. I think they had been blackberrying among the pines. There were certainly plenty there.

Thursday was my lifeguard training night in Wells, so I walked back up to the town along Sluice Creek. Before leaving, I pulled a small oil-lit storm lantern up the mast to guide me back in the dark. After the swimming session I retired to the Crown for a well-earned pint. I ordered beef stew with dumplings, and when it came there was enough for three people. Needing to put back what the day had taken, I was soon outside it. Feeling replete, I walked back down to Ralph's, changed out of my warm trousers and shoes and put on shorts. The prospect of a dark, cold, wet walk back over the marsh wasn't very appealing. I set off into a very black night. Drawing the shore, we never used torches, so I hadn't brought one. The first bit across the channel, although full of sharp obstructions, wasn't too bad, as I could see by the lights of the town. But as I got further up Sluice Creek it got very dark. My eyes didn't seem to be adjusting very well, and the storm lantern looked very faint and distant. As I progressed, my eyes did open up a little but without that guiding light I would never have made it back.

Nature woke me at 2.30, and through the porthole I could see an electric yellow profile of Wells inverted in the mirror of a smooth incoming tide. Coming up through the hatch with night-tuned eyes, the blaze of stars sprayed across the sky was more magnificent than I have ever seen, with Orion's Sword pointing at my bow and Ursa Major on my shoulder, hanging above the pines like a great axe. Only from the bottom of the Grand Canyon have I seen such a night sky. The clouds of stars along the galactic plane were like silver dust. God has a bigger toothbrush than me. Many people might be-should be-humbled by such a sight. For myself, I felt humbled by the towering black silhouette of Ebbtide's mast looming supernaturally large above me, the sky behind so bright

I could see the rigging. I was awake early next day but decided that bacon and eggs would be excessive after the enormous stew of the night before. I settled for cornflakes. After a tidy up and hanging my tea towel out to dry, left to reconnoitre the channel by the Lifeboat House; if I decided to drop Ebbtide further downstream prior to leaving I needed to know were she'd float. I went into the Lifeboat House to find Graham Walker. We had a happy hour reminiscing before I had to shoot off to get through the channel before the returning tide. When I got back the towel had blown into the creek. Judy said I wouldn't keep anything clean. I then made off quickly for Wells to fetch the dinghy back ready for departure tomorrow, this went without a hitch, even the temperamental outboard ran smoothly.

Crowding along on a fresh breeze.

Next day the wind was a light SSE and it was warm and sunny, a perfect day for my return. But as casting off time approached the sky darkened and the wind died away completely. It looked ominous, and without wind I would have to motor back, and I didn't want to do that. There was also a coaster stuck in the narrowest part of the channel, and the tide was late, so when the engine began to play up I thought perhaps it wasn't the day for it and just dropped her down Sluice Creek to the junction with the main channel and left her there on an empty mooring among the yachts. As I didn't want to sleep aboard so close to the town I rang Judy and asked her to come and fetch me. I reckoned that if I got up at 3.15 am next day and went straight to Wells I would arrive with the tide. This proved to be startlingly accurate, as I got out of the car I could hear it pouring in. I rowed across and into the mouth of Sluice Creek and then just let the tide take me. I hurtled along faster than I could run, and as I approached to come alongside realised I'd only get one shot. If I missed I would not have been able to row back against such a flow. It was a perfect night to do it, a good moon and a brisk SW breeze. By the time she was fully rigged and ready to go it was 4.30 a.m. I had put my 5 horse auxiliary outboard on the stern as back-up in case the main engine faltered. I started it and put it in gear but it had no visible effect. I started the main engine, put her hard ahead, rushed forard let go and I was underway, only at a walking pace but moving.

Once clear of the wind shadow and heading down the channel, the sails filled. Even with two engines and pulling sails, the west bank only slowly crept by, but Ishy skating about all over the place astern showed our speed through the water. Unlike Blakeney, the Wells buoys are mostly lit and those that were not I picked out easily with my Varilamp. I set course and maintained it with the lights of the radar installation at Kelling. Ebbtide wasn't a racing yacht but she would go with a good breeze and that's what I had. She fairly raced along. I attached the jib sheet opposed to an elastic bungee on the tiller and when I was satisfied they were working, as they should went below for some breakfast. Warmed by the engine and lit by the soft glow of the oil lamps, the cabin was very cosy. It seemed surreal to be eating breakfast at such speed and in such comfort two miles out to sea in the dark. It didn't get light enough to see much till 6.am and by then I was coming in on a course for the Pit, as it was such a large tide I didn't need to go to the east to the harbour mouth but continued on straight over the west sands. I didn't have to alter course once; the wind and the tide conspired with luck to bring me right up to my mooring with no hand on the tiller. A perfect ending to some lovely days.

24 The Riddle of the Sands

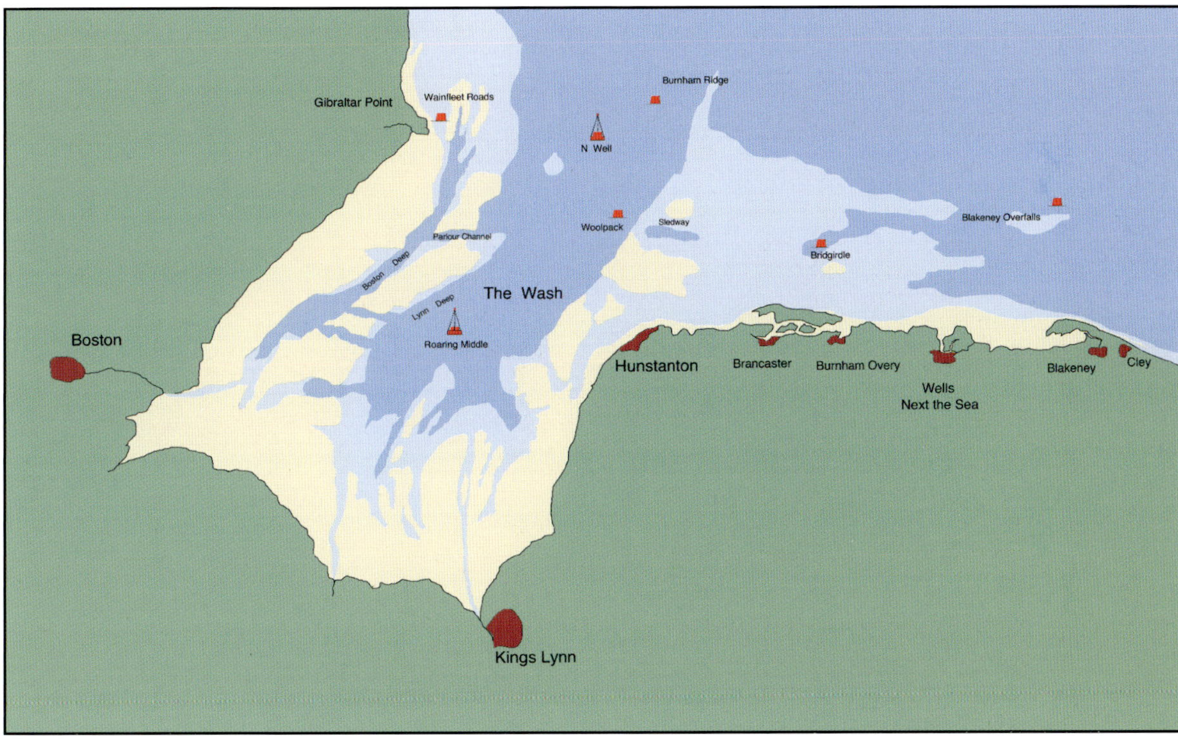

Wainfleet, tucked under the eyebrow of the Wash near Skegness, had been a tempting destination ever since I bought Ebbtide. Several times I had planned to go but had been stopped by bad weather. Dick Allen, a friend since childhood, had just completed a coastal navigation course and was keen to test his skills; so we agreed he might set them against the sandbanks of the Wash. Boston, where I had been earlier in the year, is a perfect day-sail from Blakeney. Leaving around 8.30am and with a fair wind, the mouth of the Witham that leads up to Boston can easily be fetched by 5.30pm. Wainfleet was not quite so far but it promised us some good sailing in the Boston Deep while we waited for the tide to allow us in. The channel that runs out at Wainfleet is just a small creek that at low water empties itself out across a muddy slope, so conditions need to be good to get in. The forecast was for a hot day, which raised some concern about strong sea breezes. These would make our destination a lee[1] shore.

It was a beautiful day. There was very little wind to start with, so we motor-sailed as far as Holkham Bay. As we passed the Bridgirdle buoy, the wind picked up a little and we began to make better progress. I always plot my sails on the chart the night before, which gives me some idea (if the weather matches the forecast) of where I will be at any given time, and I always note transits as I go along. The approaches to the Wash are difficult. With sandbanks extending a long way to the north on the east side of the entrance, our course took us into the Sledway, a narrow but slightly deeper channel that would bring us out by the Woolpack Buoy. We were right on time and had enough depth to comfortably negotiate our way through. Comfortably, that is, for sailors used to shallow water. A west coast sailor would have been having kittens clipping along in little more than a fathom. As we emerged into open water, the tide pouring out of the Wash was a torrent. I'd plotted a course for the Parlour Channel, which would take us through Long Sand and the Inner Dog's Head into the Boston Deep, then on to Gibraltar Point. But I had not bargained on such a powerful cross current. In coastal navigation one always has to estimate some leeway due to windage, usually only a degree or two. In this case I had to estimate almost 30° of leeway due to tideage.

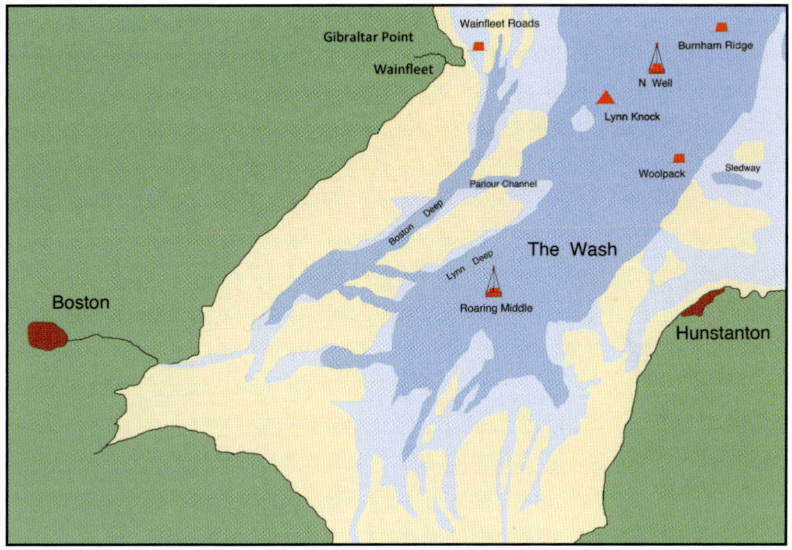

My quite large guesstimate turned out to be spot on. Eventually the buoys marking the eastern entrance to the Parlour Channel came up in perfect position, and as it was clearly buoyed we made our way through with little anxiety. We'd solved the riddle of the sands. Living so much of one's life in a tidescape does give an advantage when navigating in shallow waters. Seeing Blakeney harbour, particularly the mussel beds, being constantly covered and uncovered by the tide, and observing how the water's surface echoes what lies beneath, makes it easier to read less familiar waters. We then enjoyed one of the best afternoon sails I'd had. The breeze had become fresh, and we fairly flew along in the shelter of the sandbanks to the east. We were enjoying it so much that I hadn't stopped to think about what conditions would be like when those sandbanks went under and we had to get into a small creek with so much onshore wind. When I did, and looked away to the northeast beyond the sandbanks, I could see a ribbon of very white water all along the horizon. It was time to go. The first plan was to return to Blakeney, and so we made our way north up the Deep to get back into the Wash. But the Deep quickly became a shallow, and in any case the seas we could see ahead were intimidating. So we did an about-turn and headed for Boston.

As I have said Ebbtide was not a quick boat, but the run down the Deep to Boston was the fastest I ever had with her. The fresh north-east wind and tide running hard put us over the ground at a good nine knots. By the time Dick read off the navigation marks we should be seeing they had already dropped astern. As we approached the Witham we were going to run out of the shelter Long Sand had been affording us, and would be in some seriously big seas running in on our port side from the outer Wash. But as usual the script was hastily rewritten. Our arrival coincided perfectly with a large ship coming through, which gave us shelter. We continued alongside her for a while but slowly she drew ahead and preceded us up the river. The day was well on by the time we got up to Boston, so we stowed everything away and went to find somewhere to eat. It had been a day of very good sailing.

Dick Allen

Next morning while we were having breakfast in the cockpit I remembered being tied up to that same jetty a couple of years before. I was having breakfast on a fast rising tide, and noticed that Ebbtide wasn't floating. The water was slowly coming up her sides as she sat rigidly firm. I guessed she was sitting deep in the soft mud formed by the fine silt that comes down the Witham off the fenlands, and felt sure she would float free eventually. But she didn't. Higher and higher the water came, until it was coming through the toe rails and over the side decking and we were a couple of inches away from having it pour into the cockpit. I realised then that it was not just a case of being sunk in the mud. Ebbtide had a complicated keel arrangement of a heavily weighted central keel and two bilge keels. I guessed they had created a vacuum that was holding us down. I jumped up, ran forward and stood on the bow, and immediately she bounded free. There is nothing like yachting for creating the unexpected. After that trip I had two wings fitted to the bilge keels, which not only stopped that from happening again but also made her sail better. So there were no such problems that morning, though we woke to quite a lot of wind – so much that I really should have called it off there and then. But I'd been stormbound so many times that I really wanted to get back to Blakeney if we possibly could. After breakfast we set off down river. We'd gone no distance when we met a Pilot boat, which slowed, and whose skipper called out, "You'd have to be mad to stick your nose out there today". So that was that. We went back up to Boston.

It was a week before things settled down enough for us to go back. Even then, the weather window was for just one night, but it promised to be a lovely night and I do like overnight passages. We got away from Boston at about 9.45pm. As we motored down river we passed a ship coming up, and I saw a very black face with extremely white teeth beaming at me out of a porthole. Better than a black cat, I thought. When we were clear of the mouth of the Witham I threw the distance log over and looked up to behold a glorious sunset behind Boston Stump.

Once we were clear I gave Dick the tiller and used his mobile phone to call Judy. It would seem quite normal now, but then it seemed very strange to be sitting on the foredeck in the middle of the Wash, having a conversation in which I didn't have to keep saying 'Over'. We were flying. With the sails, the engine and the tide we left the Boston Number One and reached the Roaring Middle – what brilliant names these buoys have – in 35 minutes, gliding through a moonlit sea gilded by the lights of Hunstanton. The leg from there to the Woolpack was long, but its red flashing light came up in just the right place and we altered course through the Sledway for home. Between the Woolpack and the Bridgirdle was the darkest part of the night. I managed a little sleep and at about 3 am the Bridgirdle loomed up out of the morning mist dead ahead. The wind had become light, but with engine and sails we made good progress for the last part of the trip. It was after high water as we came up through the harbour, which was something of a disappointment. With spring tides I had hoped to continue up to Cley and the distinction of being the last vessel to make passage there from Boston. It was not to be that day, but we did it a few days later, so we can claim to have been the last vessel to have made that passage.

---

1. A lee shore is when the wind is blowing onshore. It can be difficult if you are relying on sails to get you clear.

25 The Coast on Foot and Paw

Boots with me in the Highlands

The idea of a walk from Blakeney to Hunstanton was born over supper one night with my friend Mike Curtis. I had been describing some of my favourite places on the north Norfolk coast and Mike, despite his intimate association with Blakeney and Morston, confessed that many of them were unknown to him. A walk seemed the obvious way to put this right.

Mike moved to Blakeney soon after his marriage in the late 60s. He quickly became a dear friend, and remained so until his death in 2007. He was one of those special people who enable you to see beyond self-imposed limits. Everything you offered for his opinion came back gilded. Painting in watercolour imparts an understanding of less being more - that true beauty is usually simple and clean. Mike epitomised this. During an evening he might, if asked, pick up a small guitar and play. If it was one of his own songs it would be a gentle but perfect balance of music and words. He was totally in love with this place, and became an essential part of it. When he died, Blakeney's enormous church was too small to hold those he left behind.

Perhaps because his knowledge of this coast was so intimate, he thought it was better to know a small place well rather than to have a wider superficial knowledge of many places. This coast has a richness that touches us in ways that places known in a wider sense cannot, and nobody knew that better than Mike.

The third member of our walking party was Boots. For all of his life this small, boundlessly energetic terrier was my constant companion – standing lookout on the bow of Ebbtide, scampering up mountains in Scotland, or trotting leadless around the West End of London. So you can see how I was anticipating the expedition with as much enthusiasm for him as for myself.

I walked to the end of the Close that morning, sat on the bank and waited for Mike. I thought I could hear him coming but it was a local man who came lurching round the corner, pulled by his large black Labrador. He leaned back on the lead, looked at me with a slightly puzzled expression, and said, "Whatayer goin on a hike"? I replied that I was. "I dorn't much like the look a that." He jerked his head toward the south-west, where there was a cloud. "Still, I'll say namore." It was his habit to append all his statements with these safety-catch phrases, and I suppose that is quite natural if every prediction you have ever made has failed to materialise. So I was considerably heartened by his observation. I have always thought that a person's intellect can be judged by how far and how clearly they can see down the road ahead, and I knew I was talking to someone for whom life's every moment came as a surprise. When Mike arrived I told him why I thought it would be a bright, sunny day.

It was grey and cool as we set off from the Mash Green, but my reading between the isobars of the previous night's forecast made me confident we were in for a lovely day. The first mile was uneventful. Boots had the most excitement, trying to mate with a large Red Setter bitch. Reaching the Greens at Morston, my right knee gave way and I fell. Lying face down and peering through the wet grass, Brancaster suddenly looked a long way off. My knee had been a problem for a day or two, but when I got up I found the nagging ache had gone and everything suddenly looked brighter. The path from Morston to Stiffkey Freshes is one of the most beautiful on this coast. The white of the Point dunes stood out brightly that day against the wind-darkened ribbon of the Pit, with Wells East Hills to the north west. Some horizons excite you as to what might lie beyond. The East Hills do that; it's a landscape that pulls you onward. Stiffkey Freshes came next.

They have a special place in the heart of my family. Every summer evening when the children were small, if the tide and weather were right we would be there, the children running naked, flinging themselves off the mud ledges into the warm incoming tide. I would go out and catch a few mackerel which we would then cook on an old fire grate propped up on stones. It is still in the bushes there somewhere. Those days are long gone, but I like the idea of the grate still being there, a waymark in my life.

At Stiffkey we met Jack Rowe – an old bait-digging mate – gathering hay at the bottom of the Greenway. "What about that day you raced my tractor through the village?" he said. "Left my old Fergie for dead." "No running today," I said." I just hope I can keep walking." Just after that we came to the Whirly Gig[1], another favoured spot where the children learned to ride their bikes around its smooth tarmac circle. It was here that we noticed an elderly lady up ahead with her dog. She was dressed as if for shopping in the West End – long smart coat, grey stockings and big shiny black shoes, each one of which looked at least as heavy as my pack. We thought we had been getting along at a good pace, but we couldn't keep up with her. We increased our stride but she still didn't get any closer. Then, as if sensing our struggle, she stopped and turned to wait for us. She turned out to be Scots and I guessed she could easily have walked from Scotland. Breathlessly Mike said, "We couldn't catch up with you," "Ah weel," she replied, "ye dinna do it all the time like me." I wondered, how did she know that? While she was distracted with her dog, which Boots's unwanted attentions had driven into the hedge, we seized the opportunity to get ahead of her. But the occasional glance back suggested we were walking on the spot until she turned for home.

By now we could see Wells across the marsh, but first we had to negotiate a very overgrown stretch of grass and scrub where we got wet feet. Emerging from here, we came onto the bank directly east of Wells that reclaims what was once a finger of tidal estuary stretching inland as far as Warham. The old saltwater creeks can still be seen winding though the farmland. We came into Wells through the whelk sheds, which afforded a perfect, unspoiled preface to the town. Sadly it's not that way any more.

The sun felt good on our backs as we made our way down the bank toward the Lifeboat House. The day had become so pleasantly warm that halfway down we had a break, and I sketched while we sat. I spent about 30 minutes trying to capture the scene – wind on the water and the bright contrast between indigo pines and ochre sand. I failed, but others were succeeding. At least 30 windsurfers were zipping up and down, and several colourful Sharpies were racing out in the channel at high speed. With quite a few holidaymakers still around, it had a busy feel after the solitude we'd had up till then.

Coming off the bank, we had a short debate as to which way to go. Through Abraham's Bosom or straight onto the beach to enjoy the beach huts? We went straight on. I think for a stranger coming over the ridge, the beach huts would be a surprise. There are so many, stretching away in a line as if poised for the gun to race down to the sea. Then it would have been a sprint. Now it would be a distance race. Their line decays gently to the west - first a slight decline in their appearance and upkeep and ending with just four posts sticking out of the sand. As the dunes and pines gradually unfolded on our left, the great sweep of Holkham sand flats came into view, the curve of the shoreline carrying the eye smoothly to Scolt Head in the far distance. The transient cloud shadows continually altered the perspective. One moment the bay would seem close enough to touch. Then, as the middle ground darkened, they receded to distant tree-clad hills that could have been miles away. I have known that beach for years, and it has never been the same twice. Our passage over its expanse seemed slow, but the walking was firm and we made our best progress here travelling in a straight line.

As we walked, I reflected on the ways I had known it – in all seasons, day and night, from warm summer nights in the sea up to my chest on the end of a trout net, to snowy gale-swept days on the end of a bait fork, and a fishing incident that had explained an old story. Billy Long told how just after the war a shipmate of his from London came to stay and he took him netting on the shore. Wading into the shallows, his friend stood on a flounder that buckled under his foot. It gave him such a fright that his legs gave way and he collapsed into the water, something we thought could happen only to a landsman. Many years later when fishing with Stanley, I was pulling a net on this beach on a warm, still and starry night. I had been walking slowly backwards for a long time, moving with a steady, dreamy rhythm, lost, a star field of phosphorescence swirling in my wake and the real thing blazing above me, its splendour available only to night-attuned eyes. Suddenly there was a huge snort as a seal surfaced right alongside me. My legs gave way and I was floundering, unable to stand as the chest waders filled, and I was going under. I thought I was going to drown. I wonder if all the strength going out of your legs might be a kind of fear/flight reaction. I guess if a big cat were to spring at you it might just save your life – though people also wet themselves when frightened and I'm not sure how that helps. It does explain the saying, "going weak at the knees." It also prompted recollections of another day, very unlike the breezy one we were experiencing, when the lack of wind had given the sea such a glassy smoothness that my eye could slide down the sky from its zenith to the sea washing my feet, and nowhere detect a horizon. I had tried to paint it using seawater but had been foiled by Boots. Excited by the feel of sand under his paws, and frustrated by my staying still for so long, he began to run round and round me, faster and faster, spraying sand all over me and ruining the sketch.

I remembered the time spent digging there with Mike Bennett. When I was thirty-four I gave up smoking and started to run. Every morning before work in the studio I would run three or four miles, but at the weekend I would run along what is now the Coast Path to Holkham. On days when I felt good, I would go on to Overy Harbour mouth. On one such occasion I discovered a large area of wormcasts. At the time I was digging at Stiffkey, and having to work hard for all I got, so this new find seemed like a gift from heaven. It was going to need two of us to get at them, though. They were under water and we would have to dam and bail. Otherwise it was perfect. We could cycle along the track behind the pines and then just walk through the dunes and be there. We then spent several enjoyable weeks getting good bait in good time – one of the few occasions I got some enjoyment from bait-digging.

Thinking, talking and walking go so well together. Ideas bounce and back and forth, the passing scene offers inspiration to brains benefiting from an increased supply of oxygen. We had the most wonderful banter for the whole journey. Imagine sitting in a room with a person for an entire day – how long could you keep talking? We both felt fatigue in our legs, and across that expanse even a good stride doesn't move the scenery past very quickly. But eventually we left the flat walking of the bay and made our way through the dunes. This called for increased effort. Struggling up even the smallest of them came hard on the legs. Nevertheless, we climbed the highest of them for a better view. What we got was a surprise. The sand that had stung our faces as we climbed should have been a clue. When we reached the top, we saw that the whole dune had become an enormous blowout, a whirling cauldron of sand, a particulate hurricane with a calm centre of exposed pebbly beach at the bottom. Bits of wood, long entombed in the dune, were exposed along one side, while the other, blurred by a fast moving veil of sand, was perfectly smooth. As we watched we could see this otherwise impassive countenance occasionally slip into small avalanches which, when they reached the bottom, were whipped away on the wind. We wondered how long those bits of wood had been there. They looked like ship's timbers. If they were, then the first Elizabethans may well have shaped them.

From that high dune, as we settled for our lunch, we were looking out over the reaches of Overy marshes, a restful spread of soft colours, all in a minor key. We had brought beer and sandwiches, and I had a large piece of cheese for Boots, which he loves. But while we enjoyed our lunch and Boots carefully hid his cheese (so much for canine intelligence) everything was suddenly put into a strange counterpoint by the appearance of a man wearing nothing but paisley-patterned underpants and clutching a lady's handbag. He stood in plain view on the top of a dune, giving the appearance of not having seen us but clearly wanting us to see him. I suppose he could have been some unfortunate who had been stripped of his clothes by bandits, but I don't think so. I now realise that he was one of the first of the gay nudists that now strut that stretch of beach.

The usual view of Boots

We then lay back to soak up the sun. It felt like life pouring into me. Before moving on we had a last look round from the top of the blowout. In all directions it was beautiful. Inland to the south-west was the imposing headland behind Brancaster. To the south, a multi-hued patchwork of fields bright in the sun, little woods and ribbons of hedge and, in the distance, Holkham Park. Another half-turn revealed a beautiful crescent of sea and sand sweeping away up to Wells Harbour to the north-east, and the green meadows of the reclaimed marshes. Two quite separate landscapes divided by the dark band of pines, yet sewn together by the cloud shadows that chased each other across both. In all ways this was the high spot of the journey. We were both a bit cramped as we resumed, but the aches eased as we made our way down the slope onto Overy Bank. Behind it a path offered a brief respite from the wind and provided firmer going, so our pace quickened. The pines gradually receded northward to reveal a very tiny Blakeney Church, some justification for our tired legs.

Sticking to the coast path would have taken us back into Overy Staithe, which didn't appeal, so we decided to cut straight across the harbour to Brancaster sea bank. The crossing was easy and the cool water felt good on hot aching feet. Once through the channel there is a good path along the marsh head to the sea bank, one of many that crisscross this tidescape. When we were about

half-an-hour from our night-stop at Dial House, we stopped and rested. Here Boots joined me, resting his head on my stomach as we lay in the grass, catching the last of a dying breeze and feeling at one with the world. When we set off again the fresh breeze that had accompanied us all day had dropped completely. The view across Brancaster Harbour was so clear, and the incoming tide so smooth, it looked as if you could skate on it. Skirting the edge of the marsh we at last came up to the staithe, and here we met Ernie Loose and Gordon, a hand on the shoulder and a welcoming smile. Jack Rowe at the start, Ernie at the finish – a walk bookended by friends. We were to sleep in the bunkhouse at Dial House, home of the warden, Richard Lowe. After being welcomed by Roz, his wife, we collapsed onto our bunks and conversation lapsed for the first time since leaving Blakeney. I gave Boots a whole tin of dog food as a reward for so tirelessly being Boots, showered the tiredness from around my eyes, and we went to eat.

The day's beautiful weather set with the sun, so in the rain's early gathering of night we made our way across the road to the Jolly Sailors. There was a strong feeling of remoteness, a foreignness like being being far from home. It is only 16 miles by road but we are so used to travelling faster so that after a whole day's travelling my subconscious was putting me many miles away. This illusion was so strong that when I went to ring Judy I had a handful of coins ready for a call that only needed one.

Day 2

Next morning while we were having breakfast a friend of Richard's came in. He looked a little surprised to find a crowd so early, and managed to put our backs up very quickly by inferring from our conversation (which he had joined halfway through) that we had been patronising to one of the locals the night before. I guessed his reaction was more to do with a slightly sniffy resentment at our being there, his not knowing who we were and wanting to demonstrate how in his relations with the locals he managed to restrain his condescension. None of this managed to spoil a lovely breakfast. Mike, not knowing that Richard and Roz used milk from their own goats, filled his bowl to the top with muesli. The milk's origin dawned at the moment Roz proffered it. "No no no, that's fine," he said. "I like it just as it is." Then the struggle began as spoon after spoon of dry muesli went in. It was just a shame that the little bits stuck all around his mouth gave his heroic effort away. He said afterwards that he was afraid to say anything in case he was sent out to milk the goat. Time was getting on when we finally got under way. The first mile or so was a mixture of mud and wet grass, with just a few sleepered stretches through the worst of it. The path wound its way between marsh and mainland until it came to the beach road from Brancaster Town. Crossing this takes advantage of housing access to bring you onto the bank that leads down to the Golf Club. Just before this, the path is flanked on the left by a large and naturally untidy expanse of reedbed, osier and fen, and on the right by a modern bungalow. Surrounded by wilderness, it looked to be afloat.

We were soon down to the slightly surreal aspect of Brancaster beach with its perspective shoot along the tiered sea wall and the monumental timbers standing on end all over the shore – an unintended precursor of Anthony Gormley's Blackpool figures. As it was quite a small tide I felt sure that we would find a way through Titchwell Creek and continue along the shore. But that idea quickly evaporated when we got there. It looked very deep and wide. We spent some time selecting what we hoped was the shallowest spot, but it turned out to be the deepest. We took off all our clothes, bundled them up and prepared to cross. Mike managed to get quite a long way out, but then suddenly he was in up to his neck and began to bob up and down, slowly revolving in a gentle ballet as he began to drift out to sea. As he came round to face me, the expression in his eyes and the whimpering sound he was making made it clear we would go no further in that direction. When he clambered out he was so completely pink that Boots didn't recognise him and began barking furiously. Dressing with much haste, we then had to decide what to do. We could wait perhaps an hour for the tide to drop, or we could make our way back to the mainland and follow the road. This we reluctantly decided to do, promising ourselves that one day we would come back and walk the missing stretch. We never did.

Progress along the road became increasingly unpleasant. The path had disappeared and we were on a racetrack. Every single driver seemed to be racing for their lives. I kept a distance into the road to keep Boots safely out of harm's way, but this seemed to upset some of the speedsters, one of whom – a highly-painted young woman – gave us a particularly vigorous series of V signs. We were back among people with a vengeance. The turn down into Thornham village couldn't come quickly enough. As we neared it we came up to a dustcart. It had a very large cab and an expansive windscreen. Inside, four or five big dustmen in bright boiler orange boiler suits were engrossed with their heads down. Dividing up the spoils? Playing cards? If I'd been Beryl Cook, that would certainly have been one for the sketchbook. Diving round the back of this we were into the lane that runs around Thornham to the north – a very attractive open space at one point, but some of the houses and bungalows along it were a bit of a hotchpotch. If only this coast could have jumped from 1963 to 1983! How much better it could have looked. The next bend brought us to the centre of this slightly meandering village and a welcome stop at the Two Lifeboats for a pint and a packet of crisps.

The pub was packed, full of people who would tell their friends, "We went to Thornham today beautiful place - we love the Norfolk coast, you know", but who were only dressed to visit the Two Lifeboats. I had begun to feel a little weary but, as at Wells on the first leg, a bar of chocolate put back what was missing.

Thornham Hard and the remnant quayside and coal barn would probably be the high spot for the western end of the Coast Path. Moving off along the very claggy sea bank, Mike started to grow as layers of sticky mud began to build up on the soles of his shoes, making him walk like a small boy who had failed to reach the toilet in time. At the first right angle bend in the bank, the Coast Path is signposted out across the fresh marsh to Holme village. It does this to connect with the Peddars Way, but we continued on along the bank to the dunes and the beach. I hadn't expected anyone to be on the beach. We hadn't seen a soul on the way down, but there were two or three figures spread out in the distance, their purpose evident even from far off by the tripods this increasingly common breed carry. This was the last leg of the journey. It would be foreshore and easy walking from that point on. Everything up to then had a common thread tying it together, but as we rounded the forehead of Norfolk it all began to have a very different feel. It may have been the light changing with our direction, or the approaching urban spread of Hunstanton, which we both agreed had a very 1930s feel to it. More people started to appear – a man with a loud radio, a woman with a disobedient dog. None of them looked or spoke. After this the beach became littered with seaweed-swathed lumps of 'red chalk' that looked like large sleeping green cats.

Rounding the curve, Hunstanton seafront was revealed in all its untidy ugliness. It hadn't a chance really. Bathed in the light of all we had enjoyed over the last two days, it was bound to come out badly. We made our way up onto the open area of grass that fronts the building that used to be the entrance to the pier. I threw myself down, and at exactly the moment I hit the ground a loud clucking sound started. I was baffled but Mike quickly identified the source as a glass box containing an electric chicken. A bizarre ovation for such a sublime adventure.

The Whirligig

1. During the second world war and for a while afterwards, artillery practice batteries were stationed at Weybourne and Stiffkey. Mainly they shot at targets like enormous nylon banners towed behind Mosquito aircraft parallel to the coast. Duggy and I found one and made a hammock out it, much to my grandmother's disgust, as she'd wanted to make a pair of knickers out of it. Being big enough to be seen two miles out to sea, it might just have been large enough to make a pair her size. The gunners also shot at what were the 1940s equivalent of drones – radio-controlled planes called Queen Bees, with a wingspan of about 18ft. The Whirly Gig was used to get them airborne. Fastened by a metal wire from their wingtips to a vertical metal post that still stands in the middle of the tarmac circuit, they would fly round and round until they were airborne and at the right speed, and then let go. Billy had the initial contract to go out and collect them, but then the Jane Hannah got smashed in the '53 flood, so Stratton Long took over. It would be good to see that feature restored.

26 A Row in Winter

Towards the end of 1978 I had a challenging lifeguard exam coming up, which I really needed to train for. It was too late in the season to swim in the sea but I thought I might row. In fact I thought I might row Ishy, by then painted cream, along the coast from Blakeney to Thornham. The other direction would have been easier and could probably have been accomplished in a couple of days with the tide and prevailing wind in my favour, but it wouldn't have done much for my fitness. Ishy was perfect – tested many times in rough water, light enough to pull ashore should the weather turn, but heavy enough to keep some momentum in a choppy sea. I would do it in stages so that the end would more or less coincide with the exam. I took a very old dilapidated bike with me in the bows, which I used to cycle back to the car after each leg and bring home. It was given to me by a sadistic friend. Nothing on it worked, but the tyres were hard and the pedals went round.

Ebbtide in the Pit

Gathering oars, bike and other gear together for the first leg, I could see that the weight of the bicycle for'ard would set the bow down and needed to be counter-balanced. A large lump of concrete off the old mussel ramp by my mooring looked perfect, provided I could keep it secured under the aft thwart. I manage this after a fashion and set off in bright sunshine with a cool but light westerly breeze. I took some photographs, and with the tide under me it seemed the most perfect of beginnings. But not long after clearing the end of the New Cut the wind picked up. Fresh then strong and bang on the nose, and rowing became very hard work. That it should do this- just get up so quickly when everything had been so perfect - really irritated me. Seeing the hands of the gods in everything my irritation powered me on. Reaching the Pit, I went alongside Ebbtide, climbed aboard and made myself a cup of coffee. The tide was running fast, yet Ebbtide was held 'stern to' by the wind, and the dinghy was tossing wildly in the chop. It was not going to get any easier. Warmed and refreshed by the coffee and the short break, I pressed on into the wind and spray. Eventually I reached Stiffkey Freshes, where I left the dinghy and cycled home. Not an easy start, but it would be the pressure put on me by the elements that would give me the fitness I was after.

Friday 4th November : Freshes to Stiffkey

On a lovely afternoon, I drove to White Bridges and cycled down the track to the Freshes. The tide had about 45 minutes to flow, with high water at mid afternoon. I put the bike in the bows and pushed off with a gentle south-easterly breeze to take me on my way. It was quite perfect. I had only gone a short way down the creek when I met Stanley returning from the mussel lays. Very good to be seen off by a friend. Once into open water, the wind increased but the sun was bright and warm. There was only one other boat out, a sailing dinghy. As it came close, a voice called out: "It could only be Godfrey out here with a bloody bike!" I had intended to cut straight across Garborough, keeping safe inside the high sands. But there wasn't enough water so I had to go further out. But as the sea swell was slight it added nothing to the risk. Two seals followed behind, and one stayed with me right until I got to the sewer outfall pipe at Blacknock. At this point it became a very special afternoon. There had been little tide against me; so it had been a comfortable row. With a dying wind, the water took on the colours of the westering autumn sun. I managed an easy row up to the junction of Stonemeal and Stiffkey Creek, where I moored the dinghy as high up as I could. On the next leg I hoped to get the flood tide under me to the halfway point, and then have the ebb carry me through to Wells. To do that I had to get away before high water on a big tide. I cycled back along the Meals and arrived home at 4.30, which, considering I had taken it all at a leisurely pace, was good. If only the rest of the adventure could be so easy!

Saturday 12th November : Stiffkey to Wells

Old Sheep Bridge, now removed

The tide was a bit bigger than I had imagined when I moored the dinghy. To leave and have some tide under me would have meant getting up at 6 am and setting off for the first part of the row in the dark. Not wanting to do that, I took a chance and left later. As I arrived at the bottom of Greenway, my heart sank. The track to the bridge was well under the tide, my best boots were sitting in a yacht on the Hamble, and so I was wearing an old leaky pair. I decided to try getting through on the bike. This worked quite well and I only got into difficulties over the marsh where it was soft and slippery. You try cycling over salt marsh when it's covered with the tide! The last stretch along the outer ridge was easy. Although I had moored the dinghy as high as I could, it was still at least a hundred yards offshore when I got there, so I had to strip down and wade. I took everything off except my T-shirt and top, and edged gingerly out. It was scrotum-tightening cold, and I was not convinced that I would make it without having to swim. In the event I just managed to grab the painter, but in doing so I dropped part of my top into the water – not the best way to start.

Coming to the end of Stone Meal Creek

It was a lovely morning and I took photographs as I went along. After about 30 minutes I went under the first Chalk Road bridge (since removed). Then the outgoing tide became strong and I had to row hard. I had assumed that the slack water point would be midway between the two bridges, and that the ebb would carry me through to Wells. But this place never fails to surprise. When I reached the second bridge, it was still running hard toward Stiffkey- a disappointment but, I was in good time. If I had arrived five minutes earlier I would not been able to get under it. As it was, the strong current and the bike's handlebars tangling with the bridge structure made it difficult enough. I then had the tide against me all the way to Wells. Not until I was west of the stumps of the old sheep bridge and towards Wells East End did it begin to flow rather sluggishly and unhelpfully toward my destination. As the purpose of the adventure was to build up my arm strength, I didn't feel I could complain about it being hard. In any case it was very enjoyable, and I passed some parts of Warham marshes that I had not seen before. I had also learned that Wells is losing out of the back door a great deal of the water it needs to scour the harbour. I moored the dinghy and cycled back to Stiffkey, then drove home.

Saturday 3rd December: Wells to Burnham Overy

The forecast was for a cool and mostly cloudy day with a fresh south-west wind, but that wasn't how it turned out. Abandoning any chance to row, I'd gone to the studio. But the morning had steadily brightened, and I became increasingly restless. I stuck at it till 10 am then cycled home. The sun came out and the cloud cleared away to the north-east, so I let hope become reality and set off to attempt the longest leg of the row. There was quite a swell on Cley beach, but with a forecast for north-westerly winds next day there was some pressure to grab the chance or risk being blocked for another string of days.

I left the mooring at 11.35, just as the tide arrived. It flowed slowly at first but, as is often the case at Wells, it soon became a real adversary. At this point I did not allow myself to think of the leg in its entirety. Instead I decided to row down the channel to where I might judge conditions before deciding whether to go for it. This turned out to be the most westward curve of the harbour, about 500 yards past the Lifeboat House. I paused there to contemplate the swell, opened a can of beer and ate my lunch. By then it was 12.30. The seas didn't seem to be increasing, so I decided to take a chance and left quickly before sensible Godfrey could persuade me to turn back. He didn't appear, but then he never does. All my life I have puzzled about this. Even now on my daily summer swims I will occasionally get to the beach and think it's far too rough to go in, make the decision not to, and then find myself against all my better judgement walking down the beach and going in, sometimes with frightening consequences. I suppose a psychologist could explain it, but I can't.

To complete this leg I was going to need as much time as possible. Although the tide wouldn't be as strong as in the channel, it would be against me all the way – particularly going into Overy Staithe, because by then it would be ebbing from the harbour. I edged out slowly with a sand bar to the north protecting me from the quite large breaking waves. This worked well, and by the time I got into the open sea I had avoided them completely. Just as well, I thought, as in the troughs the view of the land would sometimes vanish altogether.

I settled down to a steady rowing rhythm punctuated by an occasional mouthful of beer. The shoreline when I could see it hardly seemed to move past, and I began to wonder if such an enormous row against the tide was actually possible, or if the wind increased whether I would be able to get safely ashore. Of course I didn't want to give up. But if it became impossible to complete the journey, then I would have to decide just how far to go before turning back. The return would be quicker with the tide under me, and that idea was tempting. All this deliberation was coloured by a nagging concern about the unknown conditions at Overy bar. I pressed on at a steady pace and tried not to think about the distance.

The sand dunes immediately to the west of Wells did eventually begin to withdraw astern, and I realised that I was moving over the ground at a better rate than I had at first thought. When I was more or less opposite Holkham Gap, a man appeared on the shore and began to walk in the same direction as me. This seemed like a very good opportunity to judge my progress. I kept my rowing steady and firm, and noted his position each time he became visible. I could see he was striding out but he didn't seem to gain on me, which gave me some encouragement.

Slowly the angle began to change, and after about 30 minutes it was clear that he was dropping back. Then for the first time he noticed me and stopped to peer at me through binoculars. While he was stationary I immediately seemed to surge forward. He then disappeared from view as I dropped into a trough. As I rose again I could see that he was no longer stationary but running for the pines as hard as he could go. My absence from view seemed to have convinced him that I'd sunk. "Oh bugger!" I thought. "I'm going to have Graham roaring along in the lifeboat in a minute, and he'll never let me forget it."

Norwegian Rowlocks

I didn't see the man again but, as Graham didn't turn up, I guess he did eventually spot me. My rowing then settled into a comfortable rhythm. I had fitted a pair of Norwegian rowlocks (rowths perhaps might be a better word) some time before and they were very good. I thought the oars might move around in them but they didn't. Even with the best conventional rowlocks there is some movement, which slightly impairs the stroke and requires some of one's attention. With these, one can row with no more thought than when walking.

By the time I got to the halfway point, I ran out of the shelter afforded by Bob Hall's Sands. The swell, which had been considerable anyway, increased dramatically, crashing onto the beach with much noise and clouds of spray blown seaward by the south-westerly breeze. It was now that my back began to ache, and thus began a rather anxious period. At moments like these I think of people like Graham, and lifeboat services like the Savinesti, and the tiny thing that I am doing comes quickly to scale. I reckoned I had about an hour-and-three-quarters to go. A return, should I give it up, I supposed about an hour. I steadied my pace and continued. My back didn't get any better but it didn't get any worse either, and steadily I got back into rhythm. Again the pines began to slide slowly by. Cloud began to gather toward the south-west, and the breeze, although increasing only slightly, became chilly.

My gathering concern throughout had been the sea conditions at the entrance to Overy Harbour. With the increased swells it was clear that I could have serious problems in broken water.

Tucked up behind Overy Dunes

If that had been the case, my options would have closed down very quickly – too rough for me to beach, and dark long before I could get back to Wells. In the event I had nothing to worry about. The entrance extended a considerable distance east. It was easy to see and gave me all the shelter I needed. I made my way in without difficulty, although it did require total attention to the oars and the way ahead and my only regret was that I dare not let go of them long enough to get any photographs of the seas. Once I was safely in I got out and walked the dinghy into the harbour, a considerable walk but it kept me warm. I continued round until I was sure it would be well sheltered from the forecast north-westerly winds, then cycled back through the dunes and made my way along the track behind the pines. Cycling at a good pace it took exactly an hour to get back to the car. This emphasised the much longer distance I had covered by water. I'm not sure how far I rowed, but somewhere between eight and ten miles would probably embrace it. Today of course I would have taken my iPhone and its GPS would have told me exactly. At the planning stage I had considered trailing my walker log but rejected it as it would have just added extra drag. I also think it might have bumped along the bottom. In total the row had taken just on five hours. Exhausting, cold and at times worrying, but very very satisfying to complete.

Thursday 15th December: Overy to Brancaster

Norton Creek

Although not an outstanding day weather-wise, there wasn't much wind. As winter tides offer so few windows of opportunity, I knew that if I wanted to stand any chance of getting to Thornham before Christmas I had to get on with the row. Judy had the car, so my daughter's boyfriend took me to Overy Staithe. I left him at 10.15 and, without the bike, strode out purposefully down the bank. The tide was still coming in, but the time taken with the travel arrangements had delayed me. I should have been a good half-hour earlier, which was a bit of a bind. It meant that I would get a short, fast flight with the tide then have it against me all the way. This of course is how it had been on each leg so far; the best I had done was just the odd bit of slack water. The journey through Norton Creek with its rather featureless banks made it seem further than I had remembered. It was hard rowing, but still most enjoyable. It took just over an hour to get into Brancaster channel, and I soon covered the distance up to the staithe. There wasn't enough water to get the dinghy into the creek running up to Dial House, so I left it on the hard. I had a very welcome snack and cup of tea with Richard Lowe, and came home tired but satisfied.

Saturday 17 December : Brancaster to Titchwell Creek

There was a distinct ribbon of white across Blakeney harbour mouth, but it was a beautiful sunny day and I decide to press on to Titchwell. In any case the seas are usually a bit less at the western end of this coast. I arrived before high water and soon made ready to depart. The wind was getting up from the west, which was a shame. It had been quite still all morning, and being westerly meant it would be on the nose once I got clear of the harbour.

Keeping to the west side of the channel, I stayed clear of the main flow of the tide, but remained far enough out to get the advantage of the wind and made quite good progress down the harbour. With only a couple of inches in the water, the wind was a big factor with that little craft. I knew it would have a big effect once I got clear of the harbour.

This turned out to be right. Although Scolt Head afforded some shelter from the swells, things became progressively more difficult once I rounded the corner. The seas got rougher and more confused and I realised that if conditions got any worse I would have to call it off. Ahead of me was an area of breaking waves that would have quickly put paid to me if I let myself get mixed up in them. But I had noticed that there was a calmer strip about 20 metres wide closer to the beach, which offered a way forward. I could have tried going outside the broken water but to come to grief 500 yards offshore in such seas would have presented its own set of problems. I made my way carefully along, giving myself the chance at all times to run back into shelter. It was a very difficult and rough stretch for such a teacup, but it is an amazingly seaworthy little teacup.

Crossing Wells harbour with Beano in its prototype came to mind and gave me comfort. Once through this patch, though conditions were still bumpy, success began to seem more possible. I settled down to steady rowing and accepted that, just as with the Holkham leg, progress would appear to be slow. The sea state varied, with very large swells occasionally sweeping in and giving me a fright. Passing Brancaster Golf House was very odd. In the fading afternoon light, they had the lights on.

The seas at the entrance to Titchwell Creek

I could see figures inside comfortably chatting and drinking tea, while just a short distance away I was in such a wild place. We could have waved to each other, shouted even. But between us was certain death. Well perhaps not certain death. Possible death might be more accurate, but it doesn't sound as good. The waves were bigger there, and with the wind having gone out to the north-west and increasing, I stepped up my rowing rate. Delay would only have resulted in more difficulty getting into Titchwell Creek. I had been hoping to slip in there as easily as I had done into Overy, but I'm not sure why. There are a few similarities. Overy has a bar that affords good shelter. Titchwell does not, and added to that it has little depth, particularly if left late. As I approached the entrance I could see nothing but breaking seas, but I kidded myself I could see a slightly calmer bit in the middle. There was little point in hanging around so I hung my camera round my neck, zipped up my coat and went for it. Coming in was swift and needed every bit of concentration. At one point the stern lifted so high I thought the large lump of concrete, which I had never successfully secured, would drop into my lap. I had to control the boat Will Watch style, with both oars in one hand and the other held out as a shield against falling concrete. After that, all went well, and I rowed round into the creek to where I felt it would be safe to leave her. I tied the oars to my bike with my scarf and cycled back to Dial House. An exhilarating but dodgy row.

It was the last leg – Blakeney to Thornham, about to be completed before the year's end. I hadn't really thought I wouldn't do it, although the open sea legs had all been hard in different ways. The tide hadn't really been with me for any part of it, and had been against me for almost all of it. For it to have been otherwise, I would have had to have done it the other way round. The reason for this is that the tidal stream along the north Norfolk coast run parallel to it, six hours one way and six the other, but most of the time the tide is high the stream is running east. I arrived at the car park by Brancaster golf course at around 8.40, got the oars tied onto the bike and quickly set off. The tide was so high that I had to walk along the lowest step of the sea wall, which was as slippery as ice. It was in truth a lovely morning. My only disappointment was that the dead calm at Blakeney had given way to a fresh south-westerly.

I was soon out of Titchwell Creek and on my way. The wind was a real problem to begin with, but as I got into the shelter of the dunes that front Titchwell reserve I went along at a steady pace that became enjoyable. The fitness built up during the previous month made the rowing easy. As I got clear of the dunes the wind again had an effect. The sea became confused and again the rowing was hard. I had a very lively 20 minutes before I got into some shelter. A shallow low offered the temptation of a short-cut through to the east side of the inner harbour, but the water was getting away fast. I could see a real risk of getting beneaped, so I turned back out to sea. That bit was extremely difficult, and I had to get out and drag the dinghy round the end of the sand bar. Once into the channel, and battling against both wind and a fast ebbing tide, it became the hardest part, as if the overall inertia built up during the entire trip was all being concentrated into this last little bit. When I did get to the quay, I just hooked the anchor over a bit of quay heading, jumped on my bike and left.

I occasionally overtake cyclists when I'm out on my racer but have never experienced what happened on the road back. I was so very cold from the trip that I was pedalling frantically, trying to get warm. Up ahead I spotted two riders. I judged both to be wearing and riding this year's Christmas presents, beautiful new racers and all the flashy kit to go with them. By this time I was on the flat and

End of the Journey

the flashy kit to go with them. By this time I was on the flat and going hell for leather. My back mudguard was binding on the wheel, as was one of the brakes and the bike itself was just one big rattle. As I approached them, the man turned to see what was coming up behind them. From his wide-eyed expression it was clear he didn't know what it was. I swept past them, thigh boots flapping, waterproof jacket flying in the wind, and looking like a mad fisherman fleeing a tsunami. I think perhaps when they got home they may have chucked their fancy bikes in the bin.

I went back with the car and towed the dinghy up beyond the tide's reach beside the Coal Barn and came home. Wet, tired, and absolutely elated, and I learned from the adventure. The loss of scouring water from Wells Harbour was certainly one. More surprisingly, I learned that if you are careful and in a shallow draft boat, you can get in and out of these harbours even when it is quite rough, by using drains and lows that run out parallel to the shore. I have also learned that the rewards for such efforts are well worth the risks. It was certainly tough, but my only regret has been that, because I was unable let go of the oars, the most exciting bits were not photographed.

27 In The Sea

For at least 40 years I have swum regularly, mostly in swimming pools but for the last 15 years it has been in the sea at Cley beach, or when the sea is too rough, and the tide is right, in the channel at Blakeney. I swim for 20 minutes every day from May to late October or early November. It is one of the best things in my life, and for many years now I have had the company of my neighbour Paul Veitch. I think myself singularly lucky that the only person I know who is mad enough to join me lives next door. His being a mental health lawyer is also a comfort. The last of this book's journeys on this wonderful coast dips into my swimming diaries.

21 May 2.30 pm Sea 13.1°

Lovely warm day but the water felt freezing. Aches in the scrotum and wrists. I don't remember it feeling quite so cold on the first attempt before. A girl in a bikini came splashing in and dispiritingly didn't look like getting out, so I had to stay, and eventually it came good.

22 May Sea 14°

Not a car or person anywhere, and a cool northerly force four kicking up a brisk chop. While the large and closely spaced waves had not created a shelf, they still offered plenty of opportunity to get hurt. I got in OK but really had to watch it. This apart I had a great swim, albeit getting the odd wave over my head. There was very little tide run, which made it easier, but still a bouncy start to the season. There is the same satisfaction in getting ashore safely in such conditions as there is in picking up my mooring after a difficult day at sea on Ebbtide. Those that hide behind their mother's skirts will never understand the thrill and satisfaction of taking calculated risks and having them work out.

24 May 7 am Sea 15.7°

A lovely morning with a light easterly breeze although the sea looked cold and muddy and I soon found out why. It was full of 'snot' (algal bloom), the stuff that used to clog up our trout nets. It appears about the same time every year. Perhaps the NE winds forecast for the weekend will disperse it. Getting in was a real shock, but then it always is and it is

only the foreknowledge that it will feel better after a few minutes (eight this morning) that makes the prospect seem tolerable. I could so easily have got out and postponed the whole thing for another week. I expect I will go tomorrow, although with the forecast I have just heard I may have a good excuse to chicken out as the water will be very cold at Blakeney.

28 May 7.07 am Sea 13.6°

After the glorious sunshine of yesterday it was disappointingly misty today, but little breeze to speak of, so not cold. The beach was quiet. A dome tent sat on the top, the occupants sound asleep.The sea was oily smooth and, at almost 2° colder than yesterday felt sharp getting in. Paul thought he was going to faint. It took about 5 minutes for the heating to come on and then it was grand. Paul struck out strongly but my right arm was again painful, just as it was toward the end of last season. I must hope it will improve. Not much activity otherwise. A few pairs of gulls coming past, and occasionally the sun brightened the surface of the sea. It can only get warmer.

9 June 7.40 am Sea 12.8°

A cool morning with ragged streamers of grey cloud sweeping across the sky, carried on the last of yesterday's strong south-west winds, which were still gusting to around force 6. It was dismal going down a flooded and empty beach road. The sea looked anything but inviting, with white caps racing just a short distance offshore. Considering how cold it was, 12.8 is very cold for June, the sea didn't feel too bad going in and I had a great – if rather splashy – swim. I felt terrific when I came out, except my hands had become very cold and were quite useless when it came to getting my shoe laces done up. I took the longer route home with the car's heater full on to try and warm myself, but had to have a hot shower to become normal, although that may always be an unattainable goal.

20 June 6.55 am Sea 15°

The best morning yet. A bright sun and a glittering but smooth surface to the sea. It was diamond clear, and keeping close inshore away from the mackerel a three metre wide stream of tiny whitebait flowing west into the tide. A swing of the leg spawned a marine meteor shower. When we came out they were still going past. I cannot say how optimistic that makes me feel. Nicky (Ching) Moreton was there again, plus a few more anglers. Unlike them, however, Nicky was throwing all he caught back; another optimistic sign? Or has he become a Buddhist ? He does have the eyes for it.

21 June 7.07 am
Air 15° Sea 15.3°

Grey morning with a light NE wind which had kicked up a steep, quick, short sea, but as there was no shelf to negotiate, our entry and exit were without mishap. Nicky Moreton was there again, along with a few others. They didn't appear to be catching as many mackerel as yesterday. It was probably something of a relief for him to not have his fishing interrupted by fish. We spoke to him afterwards and he said he had been throwing fish back because they were too small. If only they all did that.

We were accompanied by a small seal for the first time this season. We have one about the same size every year. There is a dolphin which, having lost its partner, comes into a small west coast harbour in Scotland every day and swims with a dog. The landscape writer Robert Macfarlane joined it on one occasion and was able to touch it as it swam alongside him. Considering what dreadful predators of marine mammals we have been, I wonder at the power of an attraction that can override their natural caution and bring them so close to us. Seals and dogs are distant cousins, of course, but dolphins and dogs, or seals and humans, is much stranger.

A few days ago in the afternoon there was a small thin baby seal laying up by the high water mark, and an angler and his daughter were peering at it. I said I would collect it in my towel when I came out and had dried myself. I bent to look at it and it turned to me in such an appealing way I can only think it thought I was its mother .

As I went in I saw that another holiday maker was shooing the seal down the beach with his coat. It disappeared into the sea quickly and as I waited came up along side me, I stroked its head and it stayed with me for a bit then dived off very fast. That however, was an illusion of wellbeing as I noticed it was back on the beach further up when I came out. I'm sure it could be saved, but that would not be what nature intended.

20 July 7.20 am Blakeney
Air 14° Water 15.4°

Far too rough on the shore, so I went to swim the Blakeney circuit, where the tide was still flowing. The rough seas had made it a bit scummy and for a stretch the surface was covered with mosquitos. I passed Joe Carr going out with his family in their crab boat. He asked me what the temperature was but my watch hadn't registered by then. He'd been told it was 17°. That must have been in the previous afternoon. As I swam up the little creek, small shoals of tiny fish were leaping out of the water in front of me like miniature flying fish. Salt marshes are very valuable as fish nurseries.

3 August 7 am
Air 15° Sea 17.8°

A slightly disappointing start, with low clouds but not too cold; so a very good swim. After breakfast I went for a sail. The south westerly wind that had been quite fresh when I swam had increased to a brisk force 5. By the time I left the mooring and was out to sea it had increased further still. Under full sail Ebbtide flew toward Wells.

Ebbtide running down wind

Coming about to return and with the wind astern it was even more spectacular, roaring along pushing a foaming crest ahead. That fear and excitement is exhilarating beyond words. Later I went with son and grandson to take the dinghy down to the beach ready for a few nights' trout fishing. It was so warm and the sea looked so inviting that we stripped off and went in, which meant that coming back via the 'Green' to collect my Raulf Greenaway[1] pension I was in wet underpants. Janet Harcourt, the dispenser took that remarkably well but a couple of other women there looked less than excited. I then did the final stint on the gallery before coming home to a quiche made with our own eggs accompanied by green beans from the garden. There is nothing I could ever have done to merit such a full and perfect day.

---

1. See Holding the Line.

4 August 7.05 am
Air 14° Sea 19°

Yet another lovely day. I entertained Paul on the way down, explaining how yesterday afternoon the temperature was 20° which was only 6/10s of 1° warmer than in the morning which was 19.4° and that usually the temperature increases during the day by a bigger margin which was puzzling, but very interesting. I anticipated that today the sea temperature would be lower as last night the air temperature it went down to 13°, with the recent average night temperatures only getting down to about 18° this difference of 5° could mean quite a drop this morning. In the event it had only dropped by 6/10 of a degree, again surprising but very interesting. However, there may be a difference between the temperatures close inshore and those further out, probably about a degree. I need to get a watch with a temperature sensor that beaks it down into smaller increments, hundredths of a degree would be really interesting. I am also going to take photos of the shingle ridge each day and keep a diary of how it changes from day to day; that would be really interesting! I'm not sure that Paul thinks this is as interesting as I do.

11 August 6.40 Sea 17.9°

No description needed today. High summer. Paul was a bit subdued when I collected him but in the glittering sea with the warm sun on his face he quickly brightened. There is no better way to start a day, gentle exercise and being weightlessly rocked in the womb of the world.

10 August 7.05 am
Air 15° Sea 18°

Quite a thick mist as we left home, but at the beach it was brighter, the sun spilling through the mist to light up the sea a soft pale gold. A group of about a dozen or so arctic terns surrounded us, diving in for the whitebait. Clearly we fulfilled the role of seals. They came so close, we could see how they spread their tails on contact with the water to avoid getting too wet. They are such graceful creatures, perfectly evolved to their niche. It was a privilege to be a part, however briefly, of their activity. As with close approaches by other creatures when swimming, you cannot avoid a feeling of shame at the realisation that we are feared by all living things. Only when appearing as something other than human can we interact as they do.

24 August 7.07am
Air 15.5° Sea 18.3°

Another quiet morning, the sun trying to climb above a low bank of grey cloud to the east and a SW breeze giving the sea enough tooth to pick up the sunlight. It was a morning of cloud grandeur. High in the sky to the south-east, great banners of cirrus that might have been painted on with an enormous brush. If Paul had been there we might have had a debate about who might be holding it. When I turned to swim west, the sky ahead was dominated by a ceiling of altostratus, barred just like the rippled pattern the tide leaves on the sand. The similarities of form that crop up throughout nature intrigue me, but I think they show a mathematical structure to the universe rather than the hand of God. The swirling froth on a stirred cup of coffee and a spiral galaxy; a river delta and the small blood vessels in our brains or the branches of a tree.

25 August 7.15 am
Air 15° Sea 18°

A wonderful wallk to East Hills yesterday. I had to strip off to get through Sluice Creek, but that was perfect because with a falling tide I knew I would have it to myself, except for Keith who was moored in 'Claire.' His little Maurice Griffiths Senior just at the point where the path crosses. I had a few moments chatting to him after which it was all mine. I wanted to collect some samphire and as usual I found something to put it in, in this case an old helium balloon. I always find something. A was a super walk.

26 August 8.28 am
Air 14.5° Sea 15.8°

Wild morning, strong NE wind and rain. It rained heavily all night but eased just after 8.00 and I went. I knew I would not be able to swim in the sea, but as it was high water knew I could get in off the new west bank sluice into the tidal Glaven. The tide was at the top of the concrete channels. By then the rain had stopped, though there were ragged banners of grey still streaming inland. It was cold when I got in, and for the first time since May my body's internal heating switched on, although it took its time.

I swam down to the main channel, where I hit the tide and had to swim along close to the edge to get anywhere against it. I swam into the old channel for a distance before turning to come back. By this time it was terrific. As I returned toward the sluice it began to rain again. I struggled to get out without scraping myself on the concrete piers of the sluice.

Then panic. The pocket in my dressing gown where I had put the car keys was empty. I scrabbled around in the grass in vain. Then, moving my dressing gown, I heard a chink and realised it had two pockets. To be stranded down the beach road in the wind and rain in just a dressing gown, then walking back through Cley... Visitors would have thought I was on a pilgrimage. Coming over the bank into the wind and rain in just my trunks with the heating still on it was like a summer's day, but having wasted time looking for the key I knew it would switch off any minute.

27 August 7.07 am
Air 13° Sea 16.7°

Cool and grey after 24 hours of continuous rain, an inch in total, which made for a lot of work yesterday erecting tents along the street for our Village Party. But, as usual, everyone came and the rain evaporated in the face of such bright spirits. The wind had backed to NW but must have been stronger further north as there were some very big waves coming in. After several minutes waiting and watching, we picked our moment.

Although the watch only gave us 16.7°, it felt quite warm and we had a very enjoyable swim. When it came to getting out they began to roll in very big again, some of them terrifyingly big, but we found the bottom and were able to ride them down. Then we just hopped out and gave each other a high five.

We parked by the shelter and could see a dozen young swallows jostling and socialising on the seat.

Very touching. They are such appealing little creatures.

30 August 7.17 am
Air 12° Sea 16°

Sunny but cool and very autumnal. With no wind we could hear the sea and I should have let my old fishing knowledge rule, because that roar was quite enough to tell me that we wouldn't swim. The waves were huge, good to watch but deadly to swim in. But the tide was perfect for my Blakeney circuit.

I went very gingerly in off the Mash Green. The big forced tide quickly swept me off toward Dead Man's Hole and it only seemed like seconds before the creek appeared. I made fast progress through it up to the last bend, where I met the tide going the other way. That little creek does not drain the marsh, it just cuts through from one side to the other. Getting out the marsh was covered and it was difficult to get across the hidden rills.

Rejoining the channel, the tide then swept me back round the quay at a cracking pace, and I finished my circuit in just 16 minutes. Short but very sweet.

31 August Blakeney 6.45 am
Air 12° Sea 14.9°

At 2.00 pm yesterday the sky to the north blackened with rain and we closed the gallery. It then rained for the rest of the afternoon.

The north-west wind increased to a gale, and it got cold. With the sea coming over the beach, I knew I could swim at Blakeney but only if I got the time right. Too early and I wouldn't get through the creek. Too late and I wouldn't find it with the marsh completely under water. I drove over to Blakeney with branches and leaves in the road, and the wind driving hard ragged clouds inland. It looked and felt very bleak on the Carnser with so much wind but I got it just right. With the tide running hard, I had to dive in off the quay heading to avoid being swept under the boats, so an abrupt start.

It was a proper wild swim, being swept along so fast I had to hold course to avoid going under the many boats now moored in the channel.

The little creek was just visible as a clear space among the sea aster heads poking above the water. Halfway through, the temperature of the water dropped dramatically and swimming became quite hard work.. I had swum into a block of cold water brought in on the first of the tide. Getting from the creek to the channel with the marsh under water was difficult. After a tumble I managed by walking, crawling and swimming.

Back in the main channel it was like getting into a bath, although I it could not have been much above 15° A good tough swim.

1 September 8.14 am
Air 13.5° Sea 16.5°

With so little wind I was disappointed not to be able to swim in the sea, but there was still a big swell running in. To get it right at Blakeney I had to wait awhile so I came home and did a few things first. As I was making my way down to the low quay slip I met Joanna Reed, "You make me feel cold" she said,. the days of making anyone feel hot apparently long gone.

Heading on to Dead Man's Hole, I saw a man trying to launch a dinghy by sitting in it and shuffling about on the thwart. Did he have his best shoes on? It did eventually slip into the water but it took a long time and a lot more energy than just shoving it in. As I passed, he said, "You've got your glasses on." To which I replied, "Yes, I don't want to miss anything".

2 September 7.12 am
Air 13° Sea 16.3°

A soft morning with a pale sun suspended in a cat's cradle of vapour trails, incongruous above the lively sea. A watercolour sky and body colour water. The light north easterly breeze did not seem anywhere near enough to account for such movement.

There were six birders strung out along the top of the beach looking out to sea, and two or three others who were training their scopes inland observing the cows, which had just migrated from one end of the field to the other.

The sea was still remarkably clear. We swam well off and through jade glasses could still see the bottom 15 feet down. I could clearly see the stones on the bottom, I must get an underwater camera.

3 September 7.35 am
Air 15° Sea 15.9°

Some days are silver, some are blue. Today was wet cement, a uniformly leaden sky and steady rain. I backed in behind the shelter and left my gear in the car.

I expected the beach to be deserted on such a morning but there were two anglers' tents rattling

in the strong SW wind. It felt a bit miserable going over the beach in the rain but once I was immersed the heating soon kicked in and I was off. I kept close in as the wavelets kicked up by the wind kept splashing in my face. The terns were busy and, perhaps because my pink hat resembles the buoys they see everyday in the harbour they came very close - the closest no more than three feet away. Gradually the sky began to lighten from the south-west giving a lighter background to the low ragged clouds that were streaming off the land. Eventually the blurred features of higher cloud and some blue appeared, and the rain stopped. I had the remainder of the swim without rain and it steadily brightened until the sun briefly shone. It is raining again now.

6 September 6.39am
Air 8.5° Sea 16°

A beautiful morning, the sky full of light with small clouds along the horizon and a very light NE breeze. The moon was almost directly overhead, so with the sun on the horizon it was a perfect way to describe to Paul why there are neap tides at the moment. At 16° it was just wonderful. The sea felt so good, and with a bit of swell running some movement to go with the light. It was cold when we came out, and we were glad of the heater coming back. My feet are still cold; 8.5° is a pretty low air temperature for September.

7 September 7.24 am
Air 15° Sea 15.1°

Bright morning with high cloud and a cool, fresh west south-westerly, breeze. Very little in the way of life on the beach but plenty in the sea. Further offshore white caps were appearing, which explained the sweep along the beach – not enough to make it difficult but certainly enough for a lively swim.

The central heating soon came on and, as we swam, we swapped dreams. Other than large skeins of distant geese inland there was little bird life to be seen, or life of any kind for that matter.

It was out of this quiet seclusion and just at the point where we were both standing naked that two young girls came running over the beach, but so engrossed in each other that we were not even noticed. Either urban short sightedness or nothing to see?

8 September 8.15 am
Air 12.2° Sea 18.2°

I could hear the sea from the garden and arriving at the beach found that big seas were rolling in. I decided to give it a go. I got in up to my chest and finding no shelf I stood and rode out some quite big ones but then a monster came in and unable to retreat quickly enough I had to plunge through it - and so I was out and swimming.

While I swam some very big seas crashed onto the shore but I felt sure that if I could get out the same way as I got in I would be OK. In the event that was how it worked out, but I did only narrowly miss being hit by a wave much taller than I am. A good bonus swim.

17 September 7.08 am
Sea 15.2°

Crews from Trinity House are replacing the Hjordis wreck buoy with a beacon which has to be driven 8 metres into the sand. The equipment to do this was being carried over the beach this morning to be loaded onto a very low flat steel raft. There was a bit of swell but nothing seemed to be bothering them. The raft looked far too small to take all the enormous generators and machinery they were unloading off the lorries. The most active morning we will see on Cley Beach, I suspect. We had a very good swim, although it is getting cold now.

21 September 8 am
Air 14° Sea 15.3°

A morning too beautiful to describe, but I'm going to try. Nothing special to start with. A grey overcast and the lightest offshore breeze, but it all kicked off as we swam. Great skeins of pink-footed geese inland, huge ribbons of birds many hundreds long strung out high against a dramatic sky. Slowly the sun began to break through, getting brighter and brighter. The beach lit up to the west, and as the light crept toward us so the fishing boats caught the light, their red sheer strakes and white hulls vivid against a slate grey backdrop. As we walked back over the beach, the light coming through gaps in the cloud seemed to be streaming horizontally across the landscape like a cinema projector illuminating the marshes and the trees behind Blakeney, leaving Cley so dark it was difficult to see any detail.

Then, almost as if guided, the beam swung inland to light Blakeney Church, which gleamed like a beacon above the trees. To the east the light spilling down through the haze between the headlands created a cardboard cut-out landscape, each headland more clearly defined than the one behind it. Here it was Salthouse Church that dominated the view. All that splendour and the wonderful feeling of wellbeing that cold swimming gives. We might say that we are blessed, or we could (like many at that time of day) still have been in bed.

22 September 7.33 am
Sea 16.2°

A very blue sky, the sun lurking behind some cloud to the east. The sea was very much cleaner than yesterday and had a sparkle to it when the sun came out. A small guillemot appeared and sported just to the north of us, disappearing then reappearing and showing off by rearing up and flapping its little wings. And as if by magic another appeared alongside it as more appeared a bit further out. They all came together so quickly and were not fishing, so perhaps it was just the joy of being alive. We have talked a lot about 'being' in the world this summer. It seems to be important no matter how you look at it. It has significance for Paul as a Christian and for me as a non-Christian. Having a sense of one's place and scale in the scheme of things underwrites our understanding of the world.

8 November 11.45 am
Air 9.4° Sea 10°

Well Milazzo wasn't quite the last swim, although this one probably will be. Having been out for a while and swimming in warm Italian waters it was always going to be tough getting back in at this time of year, but I was determined to have one last swim. The beach was full of people and there were two anglers right in the way and, not wanting to walk too far when I came out, I went between them and got shouted at. They seemed to think I would tangle their lines. I ignored them. I would like to keep going and see how far I could get into the winter, but Judy worries so much I will probably leave it for now. A good cold last swim.

28 Holding the Line

The '53 Storm Background

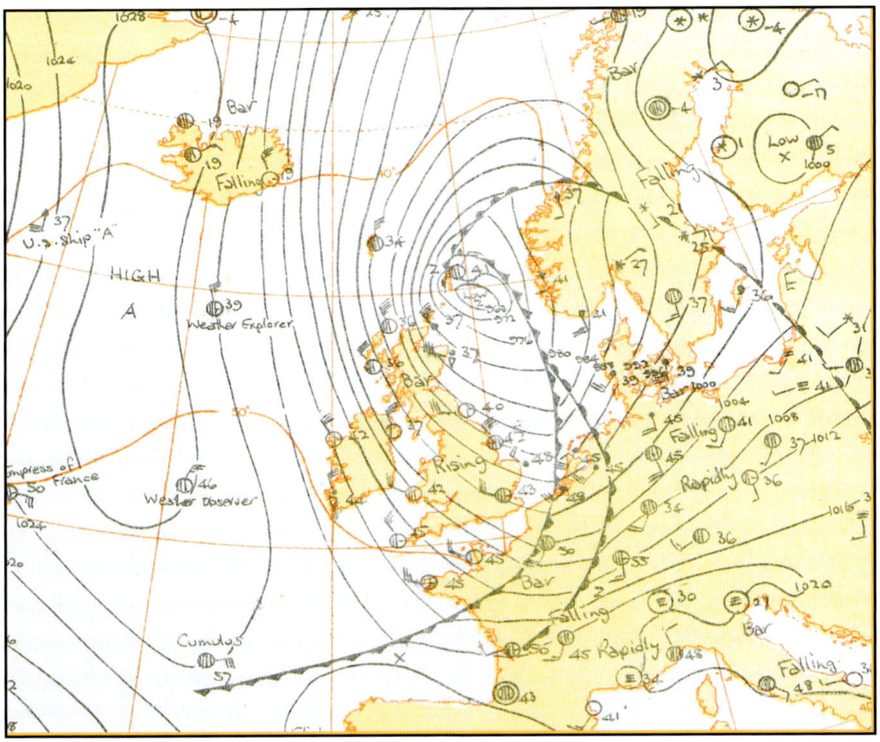

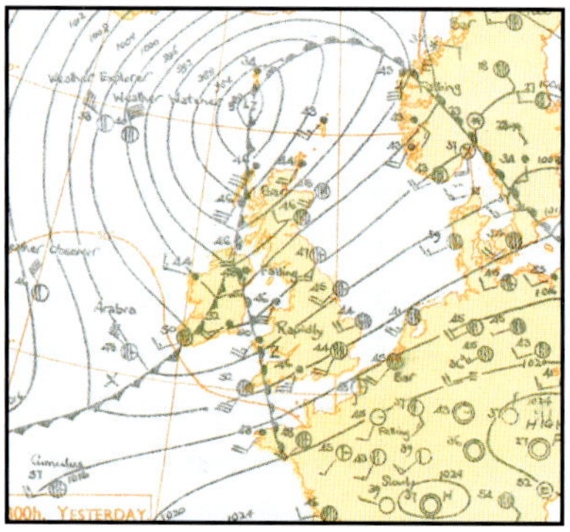

24 Hours Before

'First Rise After Low Foretells a Stronger Blow' was one of many saws I heard from the old fishermen I worked with on the Cut. Relating to barometric pressure, it described something they could not possibly have visualised. The pressure charts we are all so familiar with from the TV weather forecasts today can often show clearly what they were saying. In the case of the '53 storm it was a perfect prediction. A deep depression (around which the winds circulate in an anti-clockwise direction) moved across the country from the north-west to the south-east. Its approach, coincident with low water, brought winds from a south-westerly direction blowing straight up the North Sea. As the centre of the low crossed us and atmospheric pressure dropped further, sea levels rose by several inches.

There can be as much as 25cm difference in sea level between very high and very low pressure. As the centre of the low moved away, pressure began to rise a little and the winds swung to the north-west, increasing dramatically at the same time as the tide was rising. This was the crucial element in this event: the very fine timing that brought the wind in behind a rising tide created a tidal surge. Imagine holding a bowl of water, shape it like the North Sea if you like, and rock it slightly back and forth. The effect you would get is what was happening in the North Sea that night. A tidal surge is basically the same as a tsunami. Only the cause is different. Picture a wave just a few feet high but with a wavelength miles across. This is what came down the North Sea that night. Conditions for a '53 event are very complex and precise, which may be why the Environment Agency so far has failed to predict any of the major surges we have had. A fruit machine offers a fair analogy. It just has to be bigger – say 15 reels – and for a '53 event all 15 have to come up cherries. These days the Environment Agency tells people to run for higher ground with every big tide.

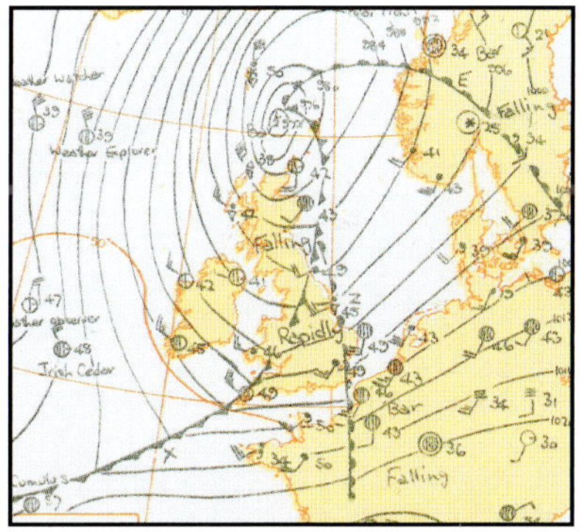

12 Hours Before

Last week we had high pressure, wind speeds no more than 6 mph anywhere in the North Sea, and a 9.3 metre tide. I got three warnings telling me to evacuate my cattle and belongings to higher ground. If they warn people of danger with every spring tide, they cannot fail to spot the next major event. But what is also self-evident to everyone except the children of the EA is that repeatedly crying wolf presents the risk that their warnings will be ignored. On the plus side there are now much better sea defences than in '53. A bank was built across the Glaven Valley just after 53 and the village of Cley is now surrounded by a robust new bank built in the 1990s, but there are more people living on this coast today than there were in 1953, and fewer who understand what is going on around them. Current flood plans allow for little local oversight. No locals will be involved in evacuations. This will be done by the police, almost all of whom will be brought in from further afield. They will have no local knowledge. Under quiescent conditions they'd be useless. On a wild dark night in unfamiliar surroundings they'll be life threatening. A couple of years ago, as flood warden for Wiveton I went to witness a North Norfolk District Council/EA flood response teams rehearsal. On my way to the assembly point at Cley Village Hall I passed two police cars parked where, had there really been a flood, they would have been submerged under many feet of water. I then went on to discover that nobody could get into the Village Hall/ Evacuation Centre because the Play Group had it. Only the police knew how the walkie-talkies worked, so everyone was getting frustrated trying to use them like mobile phones. The Cley flood warden, who was supposed to get a phone call telling him to kick the whole thing off didn't get it; so he was an hour late arriving. I left in bafflement, knowing for certain that in reality all those at risk (except perhaps for the Play Group) would be floating face down in their homes.

29 Village Projects

The Pastures

In the late 1960s the owners of the Blakeney Hotel applied for planning permission to build houses on two arable fields known as The Pastures. These fields, bounded on three sides by the old village, couldn't have been more important to its shape and character. To lose that open space would have been bad enough. To have it smothered in the homogenous brick boxes that were being built at that time would have been a disaster.

Johnny Rhodes (son of the actor Christopher Rhodes) and I were friends at that time, and he like me was appalled by such a prospect. Together we found the courage to act, and formed the Blakeney Preservation Society. There were fifteen of us including Harry Bishop and Mike Curtis, and with me in my first role as a chairman we went into battle. We organised village meetings and heavily petitioned the local authority. It wasn't easy, and there were many moments when it seemed like a lost battle. It became, as these things usually do, a public relations exercise.

The developers were able to employ professional disinformationists to front their campaign, and they had some success, particularly among some of the business people. But against the odds we won, and I have no doubt that it was 'our' victory because at that time the district council had yet to recognise the unique character of north Norfolk's villages and were giving permission for just about anything that came along. That fight was as much a benchmark in my own life as it was for Blakeney. Unknowingly I had stepped on to a conveyor that would carry me into countless similar battles. They have continued to the present day. Only yesterday I had to meet with a highways engineer to see about the removal of an enormous motorway-style sign erected on the outskirts of Cley.

The Pastures battle, along with the council's removal of John Wallace's seat, roused me to stand for election to the council. Not long after my election, another application came in from the owners for a hotel annex. That was beaten down, and then another came for a pig farm. It was clear that, just like the wind farm developers today, they would go on and on until they got their way. I had read of a small community that had solved their planning dispute by purchasing the land they were fighting to protect. Although we had the means to do this, we didn't have the power to make the hotel sell the land to us. The chairman of the council then was Peter Wordingham, and he bravely approached North Norfolk District Council and suggested that they make a compulsory purchase order on our behalf. To our surprise and delight they did, and the rest is history.

The Pastures now belong to the village and are an open space in perpetuity. I'm not at all sure that this was what the majority wanted at the time. It was one of those difficult situations where a good result had to be achieved in the face of majority opinion. I have no doubt that the village would be unanimous in its support now, but those were different days. There have been many similar victories since, but I have Beano prowling the edges of my mind reminding me of old discussions about conspicuous do-gooders and those with a need for applause, and in any case those victories are more about what is not there than what is.

Dredging the Cut

Against a human lifetime, a feature like Blakeney Point seems permanent. But in geological terms it's a transient structure, evolving from an embryonic bump on the coastline 2000 years ago. The spit has grown steadily westward and the harbour has moved with it. Norwich Cathedral is older. As graffiti carved into its church woodwork shows, Salthouse once had ships tying up. As time passed, Cley and Wiveton were to flourish, and then it was Blakeney's turn. Now it is Morston that carries most of the summer boating traffic. Throughout the 20th century there were discussions about dredging Blakeney channel but none of them had come to anything. It was straightened and dug out by hand in 1820 (hence New Cut) and, according to John Wallace, by Napoleonic prisoners of war. This improved things for a while, but nature doesn't like straight lines, and banks of sand had been building up ever since. There never seemed to be any good reason why further attempts hadn't been made, other than perhaps a lack of will.

Joe Reed was the National Trust's property manager in the 1980s, and he and I had been friends since he had dug with Harry and me as a boy. The New Cut then was completely choked with sand and we were both concerned that the limitations it was putting on the Blakeney ferry operators would drive them and others round to Morston, which we thought would create friction and environmental problems. We decided that if Joe could get the Trust's agreement, and I could get the parish council's, then we would see if a group could be put together to look at it. It was to become my steepest learning curve.

We got the agreement we sought and soon had a team of around 30 people, but getting unanimity was more difficult. In any small community there is history, long-held resentments or disagreements between individuals and families. If one made a suggestion, then another would disagree, not necessarily because he didn't think it was good idea but because that was what he always did. To stop this from interfering with progress, I got into the habit of ringing everyone up in advance of a meeting and getting broad agreement on the difficult bits first. We also had to overpower the old guard on the parish council, who tried their best to sabotage us at every step. Finally we needed to get the support of the village if we wanted to raise the money to do it.

The first stage, which the parish council and NT funded, was to clear a short stretch which could be easily monitored and see how quickly it filled in again. My role on the Norfolk Coast Partnership helped, as they persuaded Norfolk County Council to provide the huge lorries needed to take the sand away. It was at this point that I almost scuppered the whole operation. The leader, of the old guard lived along the route the lorries would take. Inventing a reason why they wanted it, I instructed the driver to dump the first 40-ton load in their gateway. After he left I tried desperately to think how I might explain such a mistake but failed; so I rushed after him and stopped him just as he was about to tip it. I should have been braver. It would have kept them out of our hair for a while. Waiting to see how this first stage worked out gave us time to raise the money for the dredging proper. A smaller group was set up for this and was extraordinarily successful.

'Big Dave' (I knew him by no other name) who was temporarily working in the village, and who had a great gift for selling ideas, became involved and in tandem with Liz Barnett, who still lives in Blakeney, set about organising a May Ball at the Blakeney Hotel. He sold advertising on the menus and promoted it into the very grand event it was eventually to become. The enormous success of this was to be repeated the following year and, along with other fund-raising events, it raised the bulk of the £35,000 we needed. The real success for me was the sheer number of people who turned out to support us. It reassured us that – even though it was understood that lasting benefit was by no means certain – everyone wanted us to try.

The first stage had seemed to work. The space we had cleared filled slowly enough to suggest that the much larger scheme was viable. We got the necessary permissions although I know for sure that our final success was entirely down to the speed with which we moved. The Countryside Commission, later to become English Nature and now Natural England, just didn't have the time to get their act together. No such operation would get past them today. Or if it did, all the money would be used up fighting them.

We had one major stumbling block already described in Rewritten Scripts, and then we were off. We removed 35,000 tons of material by dragline, all of which was deposited alongside the causeway built by John Wallace. In fact quite a lot of it, combined with bought stone, was used to resurface it, and it remains good to this day.

Dredging, however, was only going to improve things for a time. Eventually the sand would come back. What we needed was a solution that utilised natural processes, a kind of hydrological judo. It was at this time, when walking out along Pilot's Path, that a penny dropped. The first half-mile of this path is flanked by a low bank. When it was built it would have stood about a metre high and the path would have run along the top. Centuries of accretion have raised the level of the marsh around it, so that today it is barely visible. It runs out to the north from the quay, where it joins a natural bank that runs west almost to Morston creek. The penny that dropped was that this bank had been constructed to

form a lip to the marsh, which ensured that every spring tide that covered it was contained, and that all the water went back out through the channel and its scouring power was not wasted. It had been doing that for centuries, albeit to a much lesser extent in recent times. If we could restore it to its original height, then we might just give Blakeney channel a longer-term future.

Both the parish council and the dredging group were enthusiastic, but the National Trust were not. They thought, with some justification, that the view of The Point which their members enjoyed from their cars on the Carnser would be jeopardised. The solution to the deadlock was that the parish council and the NT would jointly fund a hydrological study to explore all the options. It cost £3,000, and the parties paid half each.

The engineer with whom we worked agreed with me that the bank catchment principle was sound and could be resurrected. But pressure was applied from somewhere else, which resulted in him doing a U-turn and coming up with a different solution. This was to dig out a sump (about the size of an Olympic swimming pool) at the entrance to the New Cut, which would collect incoming sediment and would be emptied every few years as necessary. This was a quite a feasible option, except that, unlike the raised bank, which would have worked into the foreseeable future without maintenance, the sump would require emptying at regular intervals. This was the option chosen, and a suction dredger from

Those first years on Blakeney Parish Council were some of the most enjoyable I've had in what the folder on my computer describes as 'Extra-curricular work'. There was none of the unwarranted regulation that we have today, and it was a pleasure to be a parish councillor. The climate of mistrust we have now has erected a plethora of unnecessary hoops for parish councillors to jump through.

Wells came and did a wonderful job. The spoil from the dredger, because it was carried ashore by water, created a very natural raised bank of sand which today provides a very usable area for people to sit and picnic.

But that initial wave of enthusiasm died. In any case, English Nature had got its act together in the meantime and getting their permission to keep on emptying the sump into the future would have proved problematic. It has taken 30 years but sadly the New Cut is now almost as silted as it was before we dredged. The ferryboats did eventually move to Morston, and although some of the problems that worried Joe and me did occur, they were mostly overcome, though the extra pressure of so many people in summer takes its toll.

The big difficulty then, and it remains difficult today, was trying to get across to engineers and urban-based council officers what is valuable in a rural scene. Trying to convince Environment Agency engineers that Cley Channel with sinuous curves would look better in a wild environment than a fenland zig-zag, to persuading highway engineers that huge metal signs were out of place in the countryside, making district council planners understand that an enormous telecommunications mast would be a blot on the skyline alongside Blakeney Church - these were the toughest because, as the next two chapters try to show, people from different cultures and environments see the world very differently.

30 Wells East Hills

The Pastures episode showed me that tackling unsuitable developments was a rearguard action. To be effective one had to be on the inside, involved in making the policies that would determine whether such proposals should be made in the first place. Being on the council offered a platform, and I soon had a seat on the National Trust's Management Committee, later to become the Blakeney Area Advisory Group. Soon after that I was elected to the Norfolk Coast Project (now Partnership), where I represented the central parishes alongside representatives from the western and eastern sections of the North Norfolk Coast Area of Outstanding Natural Beauty. The Partnership's main purpose was to provide policy guidance to local authorities so that future development might reflect its value as an AONB. Since the beginning it has had just two project officers. Both became my friends.

Over the years they and their teams have been excellent. During my term, however, they seemed to suffer at the hands of their overbearing local authority parents. It was a big idea handed over to small people, bureaucratic administrators with no concept of what is valuable outside a city. The idea of involving representatives from along the coast was supposed to make use of local knowledge and opinion. At first they got that wrong by co-opting three recent incomers whose professional qualifications chimed with the county council's officers but who had no background or connection with the place. The uproar this provoked led to an election, and this was how I became the representative for the central parishes, from Wells to Mundesley.

One of the first things I became involved with was a Landscape Assessment for the coast. It was thought that, being an artist, I might bring something to the illustrative side of it. I enjoyed this, and the final booklet looked good. But it took a long and in parts muddy route to completion. Various 'specialists' had written its different sections, but it lacked any account of the actual landscape. This wasn't altogether a surprise, as landscape is very difficult to describe. Nevertheless, I thought there should have been some recognition of why it had been designated an AONB. By this time the whole thing was coming down to the wire. To try and include something in time, I drafted a new short section. In it I described the importance of the sky in such a wet landscape, the space and long views, the role of the elements and the clean sweeps of intertidal sands and saltmarsh untouched by the works of man. In so doing, I used the words "and constituting some of the last lowland wilderness in the country", headed it with my concerns and sent it in. I went to the next meeting hoping that what I had submitted would be appreciated. But one of the County Council's officers claimed that what I'd said wasn't true and went on about the Peaks and Dartmoor, neither of them lowland. I did point out that I had said 'some of the last', not 'the' last true wilderness, but he was looking down at me from much higher ground and nothing sets me off quicker than condescension. "You speak with such certainty," I said, "but have you ever been out on the saltmarshes? Come to think of it, have any of you been out there?

Put up your hands if you have ever walked out to the sea over any of the saltmarshes along this coast." Out of sixteen people, only English Nature's representative put up his hand. "This is completely pointless," I said. "You are arguing about something you know nothing about. We should continue this discussion out there, on the saltmarsh, and unless you have good reason not to, I will take you there." To my amazement they all agreed, and eventually I took all but three of them out across Warham Marsh to the sea. It could not have worked out better in terms of weather – fine and sunny with a clear sky. I took them straight out over the marsh and the sand flats to the sea, about two miles straight out. Nowhere I know along this coast or anywhere else for that matter can give quite such a feeling of space. Scolt Head stood clear on the horizon to the west, and Cromer headland to the east. When we reached the sea I rekindled the discussion. "We stand here on a fine summer's day. The visibility is good and you feel safe, either because you see no danger or because I am with you. But if I left you, would you be safe then? Would you be able to find your way back? Being such a fine day you would have to be really stupid to suffer anything worse than getting muddy. But if it began to rain hard, or if a thick sea fret came rolling in, as so often happens on warm summer days, it wouldn't just be this argument you'd lose. It would be your lives.

The tides are big at the moment and come in over these sand flats as fast as you can run, in fact faster than I suspect some of you can run. You'd be surrounded and drowned and you wouldn't be the first. Several people, some with experience, have died out here." We then struck off for East Hills. I deliberately planned the approach from the east, so that when they topped the dune ridge they would get a wonderful view over Longwater to the pines beyond. Longwater was an almost unnatural Mediterranean blue, and because we arrived slowly over the ridge it still held its squadrons of gulls and shelduck, sparklingly white against the blue. Taking off as we appeared, they brought the view to life. It was as beautiful as it ever gets, the best introduction anyone could have. We then made a tour – Atlantic and Mediterranean saltmarsh, dune slacks, and through the pines. I took them up onto the highest dune that offered a panoramic view, and there while they ate their lunch I tried again.

As at the meeting, I had to bridge the different perceptions of what wilderness meant. Wilderness is an imprecise word. To someone who has spent all their life in a city, a bit of open heathland might well seem like wilderness. To someone living in a remote part of Shetland, it would probably have to be arctic tundra. Do the works of man have to be entirely absent? If so, even Antarctica wouldn't qualify. For me it has to be wild. It has to be evolving naturally, its destiny unaffected by humans. I think also that danger lurks somewhere in most wildernesses. I tried to frame my argument in terms of man's physical control over the land, comparing the ploughed fields, hedges and woods immediately inland, and the areas of reclaimed marsh elsewhere along the coast, with all that was spread out in front of them.

It seemed inconceivable on such a day that I might lose the argument, but I had looked at their faces coming over the first dune ridge hoping I would see in their eyes the delight and excitement I had felt. And I didn't. My carefully sharpened and well-aimed points died in the sand. "In recent years," I continued, "this place has stayed this way by default because it hasn't been noticed." Now it has, and for the first time it is being managed. Only on paper for the moment, but that will change. Already Natural England is erecting signs on the marsh welcoming casual visitors. One drowning is all it will take to bring down the full force of health-and-safety. It will not be seen as the result of circumstantial ignorance. Even if it were, today we have to be protected even from that. The marsh will either have to be tamed and made safe with bridges, boardwalks and signs, or people will be excluded altogether. Natural England has never accepted that the people whose lives are intertwined with this place are a part of it. Despite a living continuum stretching back centuries, their activities are seen as damaging and they would be excluded. Walking back, it felt like a waste of time, as if I had been trying to describe the colours of the rainbow to blind people. But of course no walk to East Hills is ever a waste of time. No walk anywhere in this landscape is ever a waste of time. The following journal entry shows how I see it as a painter, a fisherman and a lifelong resident.

It's now high summer, and as so often at this time of the year I have enjoyed the most beautiful walk out along Pilot's Path. A real Blakeney afternoon, regatta bunting strung along the quayside, Gray's Fair on the Carnser. Weaving my way through children building sandcastles on the corner sand, I set off as excited as if I were venturing into an unknown land. The first part of the walk was like being at sea, the marsh grass rolling in waves as the wind and cloud shadows brushed over it. Ahead, the most amazing wash of sea lavender to be seen anywhere along this coast. When I reached it I sat on a tussock and admired a most wonderful yet entirely accidental mix of colours. Why do the combinations of colour nature puts together give us such pleasure? Even the distant pines of Wells East Hills, suspended indigo above the horizon, managed to perfectly complement the whole. The lavender changed from rich purple at my feet to the softest blue in the distance. From there it was only a short step to the soft grey/greens of the sea wormwood intertwined throughout. Add the startling counterpoint of gold and russet fescues, and the effect was glorious. It made me think of nature's other wonderful combinations: the blue, magenta and white of bluebells, red campion and stitchwort in the spring, and the wonderful jumble of bright colours in high summer hedgerows. Nature harmonises colours just as we do when striving for beautiful effects, or perhaps it is just that we

have become attuned to the familiar. People in tropical parts of the world clearly enjoy more vibrant colours. Only in England could the softness of watercolour have flourished. I also wonder if so many years of looking ever more intently at these wonderful sources of inspiration have given me a unique vision. If so, I am the luckiest person alive. And alive is the word, because these experiences do make me feel magnificently alive. But the downside to being so alive is a very thin skin in the face of unnatural change, and the inevitable pressure there now is to tidy up and regulate. To me these precious, fragile places seem threatened by clumsy children who have the best intentions but cannot see the damage they are doing.

I am having a great summer. As chairman of the Blakeney Area Advisory Committee, I get a seat on the Scolt Head Committee which, apart from the company of some agreeable people, offers an annual outing and walk around the island. This year we landed on the first lateral ridge east of the hut, an area where in the 1930s they experimented with some rather bizarre planting. Silver-leaved poplar, various grasses and Rosa ragusa all now thrive better than the indigenous stuff, particularly the ragusa. The result is surprisingly natural-looking. The poplars get to about six feet before they are pruned by the wind, and the ragusa has spread in

a low creeping form that, with the grasses, creates a lovely intermingling of soft colours. I walked with Mike Rooney, English Nature's site manager for Scolt. As we went along we found common ground in the feeling of ownership that develops when one spends a lot of time in a wild place, and how such places are at their most special when one is alone. Going naturally from that to the way in which we enjoy landscape, we agreed some parameters.

History. Knowing the history of these small coastal places, and the four-dimensional stream in which they ride, gives insights that no casual observer could comprehend – not only the images of how it has looked, but also how it might look when authority has finished mucking about with it.

Personal memory. To have lived and worked in a landscape for long periods underlines it in a profound way, and this for many local people is the source of a very powerful sense of ownership, which the managing agencies, hands burned from the constant friction, are at last coming to terms with. Experience of a place over time gives some a more insightful picture, but I have known others who have lived here all their lives and have never seen it, and I am quite

sure it could be argued that someone coming to this landscape for the first time might have a more objective view of it than any of us. I would qualify that, though, by insisting that such an observer would need to have had a long association with wild places.

So, a paradox: if over time one can absorb a highly detailed and intimate picture of a place but at the same time have that picture skewed by a personal and emotive subtext, then where is the truth to be found? I can only conclude that the answer is nowhere, and that as any philosopher would tell me, there is no truth in such things, no absolute reality. We each live in a world, a universe, of our own making. It is just that some of us defend that world more vigorously than others.

I would not swap my world for any other. The roll of the days and times of days, the tides and changing seasons give the same comfort as a beautiful and familiar piece of music. I can love it in the cold hard light of winter or in its quiet summer glory.

31 Cinema City

When I was a small boy and we still lived in Kingston, we would occasionally visit my paternal grandmother in Islington. She lived with my aunt in a second-floor flat on a tightly packed street. From her kitchen window I could look down upon a tiny patch of grass at the back. It was only a few square feet and surrounded by high walls but, small as it was, it became a magnet to me. After a few visits when I had sat peering out of that window, I was allowed to go down and find it. I remember this wasn't easy, as I had to make my way down through dark back stairs. After that I spent most of each visit in that small, walled-in patch of green, experiencing what must have been a precognitive longing for this place. I hate being inside when the sun shines. At school I wasted time staring out of the window on sunny days, and longed for summer when the big heavy boots came off, the plimsolls went on and I was off light-foot into the world. Even now I postpone office work for rainy days.

The beauty of landscape underwrites my life, and its hold compels me to look for ways to share and describe it. It is through that attempt to share – as in the East Hills walk – that I have come to realise that my view of it is extremely privileged, and that to expect others to see it the way I do is bound to meet with frustration.

Having said that, this landscape speaks loudly for itself; so it is not unreasonable to expect those who choose to write about it, particularly those who give their work titles like 'My North Norfolk', to know something about it. But so often they don't. The more this coast is discovered, the less it seems to be known. The more that is written about it, the less is said. Transient observers, who describe the feel of the place without ever touching it, describe the light on the water without any sense of the sandbanks that lie beneath, and claim an ownership they have no right to. In today's Sunday paper there is a supplement called 'Best Places to Live in Britain'. Under the false heading 'What the Locals Say' is a quote: "We used to live off the King's Road but downsizing is just so 'Now'", and a verdict: "Charming, and more than just Chelsea on Sea". I am so glad they approve.

The natural focus of the average town and city dweller is short. Their urban environment allows only a limited focal reach – the length of a street, or a city park. This means that when they are plunged into a wide expanse of landscape they do not really see all of it. They may extend their focus when directed ("Look at that ship out there") but the natural span for them probably doesn't extend much more than 30 yards or so. Even when they are looking, it is arguable whether they are seeing what is there. A bit like aboriginal American Indians, who were unable to see the Spanish galleons for what they were. I think of this sometimes when I look at the natural world through the homocentric eyes of the BBC. I fall for it every time. Hoping to see the landscape of some beautiful and remote place, I become irritated when after a split-second glimpse of the landscape they cut immediately to a face. Instead of seeing the landscape we look at people talking about it. It would be so easy to introduce a character, then let us look at the landscape while we listen to them, but I guess they just don't see it that way.

Landscape as scenery is an enlightenment brought about over the last couple of centuries by outstanding individuals like John Clare, J M W Turner and Wordsworth. Before them it didn't really get much notice. Even during the Renaissance it only served as a backdrop. But its initial introduction was, as with the BBC today, anthropogenic – John Constable's Hay Wain, Thomas Gainsborough's Shepherd with Sheep, depictions of famous ruins like Fountains Abbey. The Chinese got there a thousand years before but it was as if we had to be persuaded to venture into hazardous territory, having our hands held by familiar and comforting associations.

Even though very little of our landscape remains untouched by human activity, most of us now can love landscape for its own sake. That those people managed to convince others that landscape has value seems to suggest that the blind can be made to see the rainbow. Assuming that they actually do, then there is some hope. For north Norfolk, though, that would hinge on how long it takes for such a transformation to take place. The speed of change here would outstrip any learning process short of instant information transfer.

As I look at the vistas along this coast, what I see is laid over a mental template, a master image if you like, shaped by earlier seeing – in my case, a lot of seeing. Fishermen and seamen acquire other subtle skills, one of which I discovered for myself when bringing a yacht through the crab pots off Cromer on a day of poor visibility and a smooth sea. This is the ability to focus one's eyes without reference points. Most of us will have been in the situation where someone points to an aeroplane high up, which they can see but we cannot. Our focus will be ranging out and back but we cannot pick it up. Looking for crab pot markers in poor visibility with a smooth sea is similar. A fisherman will want to look ahead at varying distances – 300 metres, a quarter of a mile out to perhaps a half mile, and through practice can set his focus to those distances without the aid of reference objects. Having developed this ability in earlier life, and had it reinforced through years of sailing, I feel that, along with my heritage, I have an advantaged view when I look at landscape, though it is probably a disadvantage when it comes to painting it. Which probably explains why I am usually disappointed with what I paint. I seldom capture what I see. I would love to see my work as others do. When I look at a finished painting my usual reaction is how far short of the image I had in my head it is. I might see a failure of technique, an overworked bit where I struggled or a sky that didn't quite go to plan.

There will always be these things. Part of it is hard objectivity, but mostly it is setting unattainable goals, a failure to achieve what was probably never possible. Towards the end, Monet couldn't see enough. I see too much, and it makes me realise that my annoyance with the group I took to East Hills was unjust. It was unreasonable to have expected them to see it as I do, though they would probably think my paintings were a reasonable representation.

At the moment I am reading about Henry Beetle Hough, a newspaper owner and editor who lived on the island of Martha's Vineyard. The similarities between these two distant places is striking. Both are east coasts, both are barrier coasts and both have been isolated from modern development for longer than most. To some extent that has saved them from total assimilation.

But it also meant that when the 20th century did arrive it opened the floodgates as visitors and second-homers poured in. Henry had some bruising encounters and he won most of them, creating some wonderful natural places that have kept the essential Vineyard intact. But he had a newspaper and a US senator in his arsenal. My smaller campaigns here were more difficult. It becomes harder to justify a position when you are almost the only one holding it. As the story about Wells East Hills illustrates, it comes down to how each person perceives the world, which suggests that our appreciation of it is individual. We do not all see it the same way. This is probably even truer of this coast's built environment. Those whose great grandfathers built the cottages of north Norfolk's villages feel a tie with them, and will appreciate their architectural merits from a base of pride. For others of an older generation they may conjure feelings of nostalgia and a longing for earlier, simpler times. But surely the converse then also will be true.

Younger people or those from elsewhere, whether visiting or indeed living here, will not experience anything like that. Their view, one imagines, would be more one dimentional.

The landscape, too, may be appreciated in different ways. Those who love wildlife will value areas that support large bird or other wildlife populations. Those who love the sea, particularly yachtsmen and coastal walkers, may favour the harbours and wide sea horizons, the foreshore and sandflats. Botanists would be attracted to the sand dunes and dune slacks, and each of these interests comes with its own particular focus. The birders look at it through a telescope, botanists through a magnifying glass. I recall an evening walking out along the sea bank at Blakeney and witnessing the most amazing sunset. I passed a group of birders who, to a man, had turned their backs on it. All their interest was confined to a small patch of reedbed where a small bird was hiding. For any number of us to agree that a place is special, does it need all these different elements? North Norfolk has them, but I am sure there are other special places that do not. In any case I'm not sure that trying to evaluate scenery in this way gets us anywhere. Trying to quantify a beautiful landscape is probably impossible. The features that make one landscape special are often shared by others that are not. Rare or unique combinations of features can make a landscape special, but not always. It is a trap that has no way out. Unlike the definite object, it has a shifting, subjective quality which is shared among those who perceive it, and is not an inherent quality of the landscape itself. I believe there have to be common threads, a shared philosophy behind the consensus, born of a common background, history and upbringing, a shared knowledge that provides a common eye for proportion, balance, colour and architectural symmetry and, perhaps more importantly, the subtle beauty that can adhere to the characterful eccentricities that lack it. For many, these appreciations have to be taught and learned. But to some, often those born here, they just seem inherent.

Just a couple of hours ago, when I was about four paragraphs further back, Richard Newton called in. My youngest son Toby was also here, and over a cup of tea we fell into telling stories. This is what always happens when locals who haven't met for a while come together. These stories are mostly about past events and characters we have known, songlines that have been repeated many times. They still amuse, but amusement isn't their primary function. Their main purpose is reaffirmation, a reconnecting of the common threads that tie us together through time, and which until the present day were the way in which all information was passed on through the generations. These are the mechanisms by which a collective view of place is established and are vital to those whose lives are intertwined with it.

Recently parts of the mussel grounds in the harbour have been covered with sand. This occurs from time to time, albeit at long intervals, and is part of the natural evolution of the harbour. But the mussel fishermen who work the harbour today were not part of the continuum I described in Three Quarter Boots. The result is that they were not prepared for it, and are reacting as if it's a terrible misfortune that's happening for the first time.

This connectedness is the common denominator for places like north Norfolk or Martha's Vineyard. They are largely intact fragments of the past in both their physical form and in the minds of those who love them, and are part of the generational sequence. A powerful aspect of this shared philosophy is romantic. The older generations not only remember when many more places were this way, but also through time's prism they idealise them, imbuing them with qualities they may not actually have had, or may have been there for them alone. This is why I believe that people from away are more pragmatic.

They do not feel the same nostalgia for these places, nor are they reminded of anything except perhaps what they have seen in old films or photographs, and this leads me to the rather depressing conclusion that the character of such places may disappear. The indigenous community is so totally outnumbered now that what they value is hardly relevant. The new consensus, expressed through the rash of art galleries and glossy magazines, effectively supersedes the old reality.

Having so much less understanding of what is valuable here, will future generations have the ability or motivation to protect it? There are degrees of knowing, and I am uniquely fortunate in having lived here for a long time and acquiring the eyes to look at it. I have been shaped by the experiences recounted in this book, and I am as much a part this coast as it is a part of me. I also believe that a facility with mental imaging is important when observing landscape. The internal image must be clear, and I'm not sure of the clarity or even the existence of an internal image in everyone. But I only guess at this based on what others appear not to see.

I read a piece in a Sunday magazine which made the claim that you could not think properly without a comprehensive vocabulary. This made no sense to me because I don't use words to think. In conversation, making a presentation, or writing, of course I do. Otherwise it's cinema city. Working a way through a practical problem, like a complicated DIY job for example, I do it virtually first. Just before sleep the night before, I'll do the job in my head. As I pick up each component and fit it together, I can see what I will need – more wood, longer bolts, screws instead of nails and so on. Very seldom now do I encounter something I haven't already seen. Most of my thinking is pictures. In conversation the film has a soundtrack, but seldom is it just words alone. I called in during that Sunday afternoon on a barrister friend who was sitting in the garden with the papers and had just read the same piece. Not unexpectedly he agreed with it. Words after all are the instruments of his profession. But what about musicians (musical notes), scientists (mathematics), artists (pictures). Then there are writers and poets who turn pictures into words which when we read them turn back into pictures.

I told him how I'd first learned to sail in a battered old Enterprise. Set up with my Horse-Pepper-ship apprenticeship, I pushed off, eased the centreboard down a little, pulled in the mainsheet and was away. I don't recollect any problems, though sailing Blakeney harbour in winter in thigh boots left little margin for getting it wrong. Powering downwind through the Pit, I knew that if I were to move the tiller either way suddenly she would screw her bow under and dump me in. Images informed by signals from my backside showed me how it would happen. But sailing has its own vocabulary, so I was to get out of my depth later on bigger, crewed yachts when I heard expressions like "We'd better luff up", or "We're running by the lee", and I'd desperately look round to see what they could mean.

My friend only marginally conceded the point. He said I was suggesting that words were only necessary for communication, whereas the argument made in the article was that they were essential for thought or reasoning.

"Einstein," I said, "was sitting on a train when the pictures thrown up by that experience gave birth to relativity[1]." The Nobel prize-winning theoretical physicist Richard Feynman used visual devices to show his students what the maths were saying. For instance, he would stand on a raised platform and release a large metal ball which would swing like a pendulum on a wire across the stage, and lose enough momentum to just brush his face when it swung back again.

As I described earlier, Martin Ryle and his fellow scientists got around the Mullard Observatory site near Cambridge using old mopeds. On one circuit Martin noticed that the disused railway line went across the site from north to south. Checking this with a compass, and finding it was exactly so, gave him a vision of it strapped across the North Pole and a picture of the Aperture Synthesis Array, which has made so many discoveries since. I'm not suggesting that railways are an endless source of scientific breakthroughs, but I am suggesting that picture thinking is. Specialists in any field need language, words, equations or musical notes, but there is another layer of thinking that uses images to step beyond what is known.

Those that use word tools to the exclusion of all else seem to lose the ability to reason with pictures, and are consequently very impractical. How can you tie a knot if you cannot see it your head? My belief is that, to the many descriptions of what genius might be, could be added the ability to think as clearly in pictures as in language or symbols

---

1. This is how Einstein explained how ideas formed for him:
Words or language, as they are written or spoken, do not seem to play any role in my mechanism of thought. The psychical entities which seem to serve as elements of thought are certain signs and more or less clear images which can be voluntarily reproduced and combined. The above-mentioned elements in my case are visual. Conventional words or other signs have to be sought for only in a second stage, when the mentioned associative play is sufficiently established and can be reproduced.

32 Tectonics

Activity along the jagged fault line that divides incomers and the indigenous people of north Norfolk varies considerably along its length. There are stretches where friction between the two sides results in regular tremors of resentment and bad feeling. But there are other places where the fault line has all but disappeared. The dust of common sense has filled the gap and time has blurred the differences. Incomers have gradually absorbed the culture and acquired an understanding of local ways, and locals have become less parochial and possessive. Some of the most vociferous protectors of the local environment were once incomers, and many locals now embrace the changes and benefits that incomers can bring. The way people respond to this interface has much to do with personal circumstances and values. Many locals have become rich on the backs of incomers, while others benefit in a whole variety of ways by their being here. But there are many more who feel totally disenfranchised. They see their villages and their way of life being destroyed and feel helpless to prevent it. If you asked the first group if they thought north Norfolk was now a better place to live, I'm sure they would say yes. Ask the same question of the second group and they would certainly say no. The peculiar thing is that both groups would be right. In different senses, both these statements are true. In a material sense this is a much better place to live than it once was, but much that I have described in this book has been lost in the exchange. The difficult question is: how fair was the bargain? It is hard to argue that there is anything wrong with the new north Norfolk. Who can complain that there are now so many fine shops in Holt, or so many wonderful places to eat all along the coast, or that many a tumbledown cottage has been rebuilt to stand in character with its neighbours? Those who cannot afford to shop, eat or live in them certainly can, but the fishermen, builders, craftsmen and other suppliers of local products cannot.

There are winners and there are losers. But any analysis of the tectonics that created this fault line has to accept that these aspects of wellbeing are only part of the problem.

Not all the argument is about material things. Heritage and culture are also threatened by incomers and outsiders. What I would argue is that while some have gained through the new prosperity, in what has been lost all of us are losers. As I see it, the threats and damage to local identity and character have come from three directions and can be separated broadly into past, present and future. The first, which is largely damage done, is the demographic change that has seen local youngsters replaced by elderly incomers. As a force rather than as individuals, these have been responsible for much of the erosion of local culture. The second – happening now and certain to get worse – is the over-zealous deployment of urban infrastructure in the countryside by the local authorities and utility companies. Last but by no means least, the wildlife NGOs led by Natural England have gained a frightening degree of control over much of the open landscape and land-use of this coast. This is having an effect right now but has much more serious implications for the natural evolution of this coast and the future of its people.

North Norfolk was lucky in that it was granted AONB status in time to save it from the fate suffered by Cornwall, Cumbria etc. But while much of the infrastructure and landscape was initially saved, a steady and subtle attrition, driven by the local authorities, has been gathering pace. With the advent of windfarms, non-vernacular eco-housing and modern safety standards, it has now reached the point at which it could be destroyed for ever. If this were enough, the social heritage has fared far worse. The tightly-knit, self-sustaining culture common to so many small communities, which hung on longer here than in most other places, is now mostly gone. The memory of it remains among many locals, and most of the resentment directed towards newcomers stems from the belief that they are responsible for its demise. While understandable, this is not entirely fair. Its loss isn't attributable to a particular group of people or to any deliberate plan, plot or design. It is entirely down to national demographics.

The last forty years have seen huge changes in the local population mix. It may be the legacy of an historically rich gene pool, or there may be some other explanation, but the young people of the north Norfolk coast are unusually bright, and improvements in education and educational opportunities have seen ever more of them go on to university and significant careers elsewhere. One of my best friends has three sons. Two went to university and did extremely well. One of them is now the director of one of the country's biggest financial institutions, and the other two have important careers in the military. They do not live here. Another friend has two daughters. Both are doing very well, one at Cambridge and the other at Lincoln University. My nephew is a highly-qualified environmental scientist. My own children spent time abroad gaining qualifications. I could go on and on, but what is true is that only a handful of the children of the people I know now live in Norfolk. In fact very few even live in Britain. Altogether I would estimate that two thirds of all indigenous children leave for better prospects elsewhere.

This, incidentally, may be one of the reasons why many incomers tend to misjudge or underestimate locals, basing their evaluation entirely on those who did not make the cut. Under normal circumstances one would expect this exodus to have dramatically reduced the population. This has not happened because, in perfect step with the young people leaving, there has been an influx of older retired people coming in. Their arriving in such numbers has significantly altered the demographic. They have created a demand for housing that has put house prices almost completely out of local reach, and shifted resource allocation from the young to the old.

Over this same period the popularity of this coast as a holiday destination has increased to the point where, during the summer months, the population doubles yet again. The much larger profits to be made from holiday lets absorb almost all the rentable accommodation which, alongside high house prices, creates a no-win scenario for local youngsters with limited resources. But it isn't anyone's fault. It is the way of the world, owing more to evolution than to deliberation.

This being the case why is there so much acrimony? Well, the driver has to be the loss of a time-honoured way of life and a very real feeling of dispossession. Finding yourself in a minority in your own place, and having strangers celebrate your environment and heritage without acknowledgement of its creators and at your expense is galling indeed. The increasing value placed on the environment, and particularly on its wildlife, puts even more pressure on many locals, who now realise that they are less important than the birds. The huge raft of protection now afforded to wildlife along this coast puts people firmly in second place. The major misunderstanding of many incomers, which I will call the urban-rural myth, was brought with them. A preconceived and idealised alternative countryside, a world entirely of the mind, a bespoke creation born perhaps of city daydreams and pieced together from imported ideas and images, it bears little resemblance to real rural life or the true countryside. We country-dwellers are often able to see this alternative creation on our television screens, as the countryside is observed and interpreted by urban programme-makers. This new virtual countryside is a tidy place, silent except for birdsong, bathed in sea- and wildflower-scented air, a slaughterhouse-free place where the verges are trimmed, the cocks don't crow and the pragmatic realities of what makes a functioning countryside do not exist. They are not a part of the dream. All of us have the right to realise our dreams, but a problem arises when fantasy collides with the real thing. The timeless stewardship of landscape and wildlife, which has always been the responsibility of country people, throws up all kinds of unpleasant realities that offend the dreamer's vision. Fox-hunting we all know about, but any kind of vermin control or balancing of the natural order is problematical. This is true even for wildlife managers. A Beatrix Potter kind of anthropomorphism is a big part of the urban-rural myth. There is no understanding within it of how the natural part of the countryside works. Even those with an interest in some of the wildlife, like birders, do not have a balanced view of how birds fit in with everything else. The problem in the main seems to be that the countryside is seen from the outside as a natural environment, which of course it isn't. It is an entirely man-made creation that has to be managed to remain in balance. Until that fact is grasped, there can be no proper understanding of how it works.

So much rural heritage has been lost, not just because it did not chime with the incomers' template (though that is true for a lot of it), but also because their thoughtlessness erased anything that was too subtle to register through a lens smeared with romantic urban Vaseline. In the last few decades many of these dreamers have found the wherewithal not just to realise their dream in the bricks and mortar of their own country retreat, but in cases like Burnham Market, where the effect is compounded by the sheer number of incomers gravitating to the same place, they have begun to give the dream real substance. They have inflicted it on an entire village so that the fantasy is rapidly overtaking reality and becoming the accepted view of what this part of the world is like.

So the friction increases. People who, had they come here with a genuine intention or hope of integrating with those they found here, and who would have been made very welcome, prefer instead to live out this irritating fantasy, which apart from infuriating the locals, blinds them to how wonderful this place really is. By demoting local people to bumpkins, they also deny themselves any opportunity of ever learning anything from them. To see the place and not see the people is to not see it at all. Any place is the sum total of those who live in it, maintain it, and in this case whose forebears created it in the first place. It is like a Russian doll. Only with curiosity, effort and patience will you be rewarded with the hidden heart of the place.

A further misunderstanding, which I briefly touched on earlier, is how some incomers underrate locals and their way of life. With the cream of local youngsters leaving for higher education and better jobs, incomers judge all of us on an assessment of those that remain. They conclude that low incomes are a result of low aspiration and a lack of imagination, intelligence and motivation. Although they themselves have decided to come and live here because of the quality of life, they fail to see that some youngsters stay for exactly the same reason. They say things like, "These people should pull their fingers out and do as I did. Get up off their backsides and work. Then they would be able to afford a house."

Outspoken incomers, usually those who deny their presence has created a problem, are mostly self-made, highly-motivated people for whom it is understandably difficult to grasp such a simple concept as being content, indeed harmoniously happy, with a life bound by relatively unchanging circumstances. People making a perfectly reasonable living based on what the land or a particular patch of sea will support do not appear to be ambitious. Local fishermen catch more or less the same amount of fish and shellfish each year, and rising costs are met by charging a little more for what they catch, much aided in recent years by the many new restaurants that have sprung up, not by trying to catch more.

The consequences of the greed-driven, short- sighted approach has been dramatically demonstrated here in recent years by incomer fishermen with bigger, faster boats going ever further out and deploying unsustainable numbers of pots, thereby seriously depleting crab stocks. It is exactly the same over-reaching greed that has caused much of the recent economic turmoil. The world may now be waking up to the value of something the people of this coast have always known about – sustainability. Most incomer misunderstanding stems from not seeing everything. Another typical incomer statement, "This place is like everywhere else; it belongs to everyone who lives here", seems irrefutable. Surely nobody could disagree. How could anyone believe that it belongs to some people more than others? Inarguable as it may seem, as a local I am bound to try. So this is a somewhat personal answer to that question.

This is my home. Generations of my family have lived here, and I am related to many of the remaining indigenous population. We are the living representatives of those who created the place, and who like ghosts in the machine remain in its charm and character. I know this place as I know my own being. My association is visceral. This place is as much a part of me as I am a part of it. This kind of attachment, however, comes at a price. There is an emotional cost to caring for this place. Feelings of belonging, of nostalgia and ownership, bring with them a need to protect, and for me personally a terrible sense of failure in having been unable to prevent so much of that heritage from disappearing.

The following is an extract from a submission relating to a small and unnecessarily contentious planning application sent to North Norfolk District Council. It illustrates the lack of understanding of rural life by incomers, and the subtlety and necessity of local knowledge.

Dear Sir,
I am a local person who has lived in the Cley area all my life and from that position of local knowledge I would like to support this application on two counts. Firstly, that the principal purpose of the proposed annex is to serve as a retreat for the applicant (or any subsequent owners of the property) in the event of a tidal surge flooding of the main house, thereby making it uninhabitable for a prolonged period. I have witnessed three tidal surges in my life, those of 1953, and 1978 being the most severe. My home was flooded in 1953 and having lived through the aftermath of that I can assure the members of the Planning Subcommittee that this need is genuine. In fact I would go further and state that unless they have witnessed events of this kind for themselves they are probably not qualified to pass judgment on the validity of the applicant's claim in this respect.

Salt water flooding brings far more serious and longer-term problems than fluvial flooding. On November the 9th 2007 a tidal surge raised the water in Cley Channel to the very top of the sea bank that protects the marshes that front this property. As good fortune would have it the surge peaked before high water thus avoiding the bank being overtopped; however, it was a close run thing. If the surge had peaked 30 minutes or an hour later the applicant's property would have been seriously flooded. If the widely accepted predictions for increased storminess and sea level rise associated with climate change are accepted by NNDC, then they have no other option than to grant this application.

Set against all the advice coming from the Environment Agency, the applicant is demonstrating considerable wisdom in wanting to create a safe haven for herself. My second point concerns good neighbourliness. Even as a child I was made to understand its importance, it is an absolute prerequisite for harmony in small communities. Sadly I have seen very little of that during the contentious course of this application. The reason for that, I suspect, is that many of today's incomers have little experience of it or understanding of its value.

So instead of overtures of friendship, patience and goodwill, which can usually resolve these minor kinds of difficulty, we have had months and months of acrimony, hot air and hot tempers, creating wounds that will probably never heal, just because people have forgotten how to live together in harmony.

If pressed I believe most of the objectors to this application would admit that based on planning grounds alone the justification for such an unpleasant situation is pretty thin. This is a minor application that has been lifted up into quite undeserved prominence by the relentless pressure of a few vociferous neighbours and their many recruits. People who will never see this building and have no real interest in it other than as friends of the objectors, and who would otherwise behave very differently, have seen nothing wrong in gathering together to bring as much force as possible to bear on an elderly lady. This situation is disgraceful and should be ended forthwith. NNDC have the opportunity and the power to do this by granting this application.

Between the lines of this letter there is a glimpse of the way in which a lack of knowledge and a lack of understanding on the part of incomers can cause problems. What it also shows is how, through changes to the make-up of our local authorities and how they function, local people and their way of life slip off the agenda. Most officers employed by the district and county councils come from towns and cities. The majority of elected members, being mostly retired incomers, also have urban backgrounds. As a result we get urban governance of rural areas, and this is responsible for a whole range of irritants for those who have always lived here. They can range from the allocation of affordable housing to having your immediate neighbourhood urbanised by pavements and street lights.

I am an environmentalist and have worked to protect wildlife all my adult life. I have served as chair of the National Trust's advisory body for their North Norfolk properties and the Special Area of Conservation (SAC) Advisory for the North Norfolk Coast. Nevertheless I have always tried hard to maintain a fair balance between the interests of wildlife and those of people, which in most cases ought, to mean the same thing but seldom do.

Many conservationists seem to suffer from tunnel vision. This is particularly true of the birders, those eternally migrating obsessives who swoop down on us in flocks, block the roads with their cars and the pathways with their numbers, and then leave as quickly as they came. I must be careful what I say here because one of my friends is both a birder and an excellent all-round naturalist. However, I believe him to be the exception that proves the rule.

During my years of conservation work it became increasingly clear to me that this particular group had steadily and systematically penetrated the corridors of English Nature, now Natural England, to further protect and promote its obsession, and as a consequence had brought in a much more aggressive anti-fisherman, anti-bait-digger, anti-people attitude. On one occasion I was so convinced of this that I thought that the EN person concerned must have come to birdwatch on the Stiffkey mudflats and been physically threatened by a bait-digger. Anyway, this has introduced unreasonable bias in decisions where birds are concerned, sometimes even at the expense of other wildlife, something that may well be dramatically proved if the present plan to introduce intertidal MCZs[1] is allowed to proceed. Altogether this is bad news for the people who live and work here.

Along with the conservation NGOs, Natural England has ensured that over the last few decades this entire stretch of coast has been smothered with wildlife designations - SAC, SPAs, SSSIs, Ramsar sites, plus the all-powerful European Habitats Directive. These have seriously restricted what people may do in or near these areas, and have made what in the past would have been quite routine activities much more complicated. In some cases they have made them impossible. Thus they have become an impediment to wider sustainability and have encouraged a stultifying mindset. A very basic bit of harbour maintenance cannot now be undertaken without a thorough impact assessment requiring months of work and additional expense. There are of course occasions when this is very proper and necessary. But it is also quite clear to many of us that those within Natural England who have a single species agenda, and who see all human activity as damaging to this interest, will ensure that this process is always implemented whether it is necessary or not, simply because they cannot stop themselves from seeing local people and their interests as a problem.

In recent years things have improved somewhat. In particular, the consultation process that was required to set up the SAC (Special Area of Conservation) designation for this coast. The 'Guiding Principles' included these important words: "It is essential that owners and occupiers, right holders, local interests, and user groups should be encouraged to participate in the process at the earliest opportunity." In other words, a participatory decision-making structure involving a wide range of stakeholders. As a consequence, local people were able to make a contribution to Regulation 33 (the Bible for the SAC), thereby forcing English Nature to grudgingly accept that local people not only created but largely maintain this environment.

English Nature had to have its arm twisted quite far up its back before it would yield the point, and it was the amount of force needed to achieve this that finally convinced me of the existence of an internal faction with a hidden agenda. Really good naturalists would know the extent to which traditional longshore activities contribute to the natural environment.

Geologically speaking, the north Norfolk coast is a young barrier coast in the early stages of its evolution. Most barrier coasts are fronted by outer reefs and strings of islands which if they are allowed to evolve naturally. Barrier coasts and islands are dynamic systems formed by the interaction of wave, wind, and tidal energies that erode, transport and deposit sediments. By absorbing the impact of high-energy marine processes, barrier islands reduce erosion of the mainland coast and provide shelter for sensitive coastal habitats, although the shingle ridges and dune systems already do the job very effectively.

The south-east of England is sinking steadily due to postglacial rebound, and the slow melting of ice during the present interglacial period is raising sea levels. The reclaimed areas along this coast cannot forever be isolated from this process. Subsidence of the reclaimed marsh and accretion of the saltmarsh have left Blakeney Freshes up to a metre-and-a-half lower than they would otherwise have been. This is unsustainable, and one can quite sensibly argue that the sooner the problem is addressed the easier the solution will be. To do nothing means we either leave a very difficult legacy for our grandchildren, or a natural catastrophe will do it for us. Neither of these is a an acceptable option.

Blakeney Freshes is the large area (40 hectares) of freshwater marshes between Blakeney and Cley, which runs round the corner into Wiveton. It constitutes some of the very best habitat of its kind on this coast. Its proximity to Cley Reserve and the Glaven Valley, plus the sea and the saltmarshes to the west, makes it very special indeed - the jewel in the crown of north Norfolk's coastal reserves, one might say. To argue that it should be returned to the sea seems perverse, but like most things there is more to it than meets the eye. This coast clearly has some very difficult choices to make in the years ahead, and the 'managed realignment' of Blakeney Freshes is one of the first that will have to be confronted. A decision of this kind will never be easy, and there is a real risk that the many wildlife designations have the potential (if they continue to be used obstructively) to make such a decision very much more difficult, if not impossible, extending the process until nature loses patience and produces a catastrophic realignment of her own.

Managed realignment, the term used to describe returning reclaimed land to the sea, was one of eight options set out when the Glaven River had to be diverted a few years ago. Wiveton Parish Council, along with those of Cley and Blakeney, gave an enormous amount of time to the consultation process and many of us argued very strongly for realignment as the most sustainable and forward-thinking option on the board. But it was dismissed. When we asked why, and how the points for the various options had been added up, we were told that the chosen option, that of moving the channel back a couple of hundred yards, was the only one Defra would countenance. I am recounting this now simply to show that the argument I am about to make has already been rehearsed. Why, you must be wondering, can letting such a valuable asset be lost to the sea possibly be the best option? Well, it would not be lost. That is just an example of the language used by opponents.

To see why it is the best option requires us to take a much broader view, one that includes local people and a much bigger slice of time. Blakeney Freshes are very special. If they were to be abandoned, the European Habitats Directive may require Natural England, in conjunction with the National Trust, which owns much of it, to replace some of it elsewhere, although initially they would be expected to try to do that in the immediate vicinity. Some of it (the most important part) could undoubtedly be accommodated within the Glaven Valley. But only some, and because it is so special it would be very difficult to find anywhere else that could provide equivalence. But Blakeney Freshes would remain as salt marshes, which are still an extremely valuable wetland habitat. Added to the replacement habitat, this would create 80 hectares of nature reserve. Double what we have now.

If predictions of increased storminess and sea-level rise are correct, then all the areas of reclaimed marsh along the coast will become vulnerable and potentially very dangerous. The villages and towns that sit behind sea banks are threatened in a far more sinister way than those that do not. During storm surges sea banks often breach, sometimes in a catastrophic way, so what in other places might be a steady and predictable rise of the tide becomes a tsunami. Streets can go from being rain wet to being under four metres of water in as many minutes. This is the deadly threat to those living behind sea banks. Blakeney and villages like it, which are fronted by dune systems and saltmarsh, are much less exposed to these dangers. The dunes reduce windage, and the much higher marsh levels dissipate most of the wave energy.

Allowing Blakeney Freshes and the other parcels of reclaimed marsh along this coast to go back to the sea would enable it to evolve naturally as a barrier coast, and at the same time extend the same ongoing protection that Blakeney enjoys to all communities currently at risk. Using wildlife designations to hang on to wildlife sites for as long as possible presents a major threat to human life.

Blakeney Freshes comprises grazing marsh, reedbeds and some grassy hills that were once sand dunes that formed over glacial ridges. Over the 400 or so years since this area was embanked, much has changed.

The surrounding saltmarsh has continued to accrete, growing imperceptibly with every spring tide that has covered it, and is now several feet higher than the fresh marsh which has subsided. It is this, and the possibility that saltmarsh accretion may accelerate with sea-level rise, that makes keeping it untenable.

This of course is the empirical view. But there is another view – less pragmatic, more romantic perhaps, but no less important from a human perspective. We each have our own relationships with the world around us, and our happiness can have much to do with the extent to which we are in harmony with it, how beautiful we find it, how much we enjoy it through our work or play, and, perhaps most important, through our association with it over time. Landscape beauty would certainly be enhanced by realignment, but in the short term people's attachment to the landscape could be one of the great obstacles.

Many local people, particularly the older generation, those who have lived here all their lives, may not want it to change. Letting the sea back in will wash away more than just paper designations. It will wash away memories. Parts of people's lives will disappear, and that would be felt as loss. The young, I am sure, will see its potential and be excited by it but the rest may have to be persuaded. So important do I believe realignment to be that I want to try and do just that. From my gallery on the Carnser at Blakeney, I regularly saw families pull onto the car park, get out of their cars and with the children running make their way over and up onto the sea bank, expecting to find the sea beyond. They were always surprised and disappointed that it wasn't there. Although technically dry land finishes where the spring tides leave their tangle along the quayside, there is an awful lot of land between Blakeney and the open sea.

What if those children could run up the bank and not be disappointed? What if they were greeted by a breathtaking view, a vast blue stretch of water as far as the eye could see, great salt water lakes dotted with islands and surrounded by vast mudflats and saltmarshes? Sailing dinghies out in the distance would be making their way through the old channel, where enough water would remain for it to be navigable even when the tide was out.

What might be possible? A small marina for dinghies between Cley and Wiveton where youngsters could learn to sail in safety. A road again , between Blakeney and Cley, with a string of possibilities all the way along it. A land and seascape that would add magnificently to the beauty of our coast. The benefits for the people of Cley, Blakeney, Morston and all those who visit them would be enormous.

How Blakeney Freshes might look on a normal tide.

Wildlife would benefit too - waders on the mudflats, geese on the saltings and ground-nesting birds on the islands. The birds live quite harmoniously with man in the harbour, and they would do so here too.

It would offer a lifeline to Blakeney, by increasing the tidal prism it would scour Blakeney harbour, deepening the channels and allowing bigger boats to get up to the quay and extend its economic viability for hundreds of years instead of the few decades it has at present.

This benefit is beyond calculation and would transform the prospects of local people. In the present Shoreline Management Plan, Blakeney Freshes is the only reclaimed area along this coast where realignment is a future option.

Sadly it is the wider view that is lacking, this is a dynamic and rapidly changing coast and shoreline and flood management plans that fail to take account of it are certain to be washed away, they cannot hope to be effective unless they look ahead at least a century.

So I think it doubtful that this view would carry much weight against the wildlife interests. In the short term the tourism benefits generated by wildlife and the value of the coast path will out - weigh the aurguments based on the geomophology.

It was the power, money and authority of the day that uncaringly threw up these banks, dismissing the interests and wellbeing of local people whose livelihoods were destroyed through the loss of the ports and fisheries. It would be a shame should economics, politics and self-interest repeat that mistake again today.

---

1 MCZs Marine Conservation Zones

33 Dust in the Wind

My original destiny would have seen me grow up in Kingston-upon-Thames and a life far removed from the one I have had. It was chance that brought me to north Norfolk, and it was chance that saw my college education curtailed and my course diverted to the sea. I had no regret about the first diversion, but for a long time I felt my unfinished education had robbed me of the chance to go to university. But no amount of education or attendant success could have come close to matching the life I have had this side of the coin's toss. I was made for this place, and in turn this place has been the making of me. I have become as integrated with it as the Brylcreem and bicycle oil on Charlie Potterton's hands. But here my most recent life, which has certainly not been dull, has been skipped over in favour of the earlier years, some of them the earliest I can remember.

The reason, as you have gathered, is that so much has changed. The old part of Blakeney looks pretty much as it did when I was a child, and in summer I still swim in Dead Man's Hole, though I keep my trunks on now. It looks just the same, and if I look hard enough I can still see my small mud-smothered comrades sliding down the muddy slopes of those wonderful summers. But there are no village children there now, and my comrades are either exiled or dead. This is mirrored in the old village. When I was a child, every cottage and house had a local family living in it. Now all but those of the Blakeney Neighbourhood Housing Society are holiday homes, bustling with strangers in summer, empty in winter. The predecessors of those families stretched back through time, linked together in a continuity that shaped the spirit and culture of the community. They are gone, and none of their kind will come after them. As we grow old we reach a point where far more loved ones are dead than alive. I am very fortunate to have new younger friends to fill those spaces.

But a void remains, a void that was emphasised for me a couple of years ago by a dream. It was a day of village celebration and was centred on the Blakeney Hotel and the quay. The time was the 1960s, with a cast from that period of my life. It was a hot summer day and people were coming out from the hotel to cool down in the light sea breeze. I was standing with a group by the quayside, all but myself now dead. There was much laughter and friendly high spirits. Two larger-than-life village characters, Marion Horne and Jeremy Ryder Smith, were being lauded for their portrayal of Britannia in a recent float parade. I awoke with my head full of jokes and laughter. But it was no surprise on waking from such detailed familiarity to feel real grief as much-loved and long-familiar faces retreated to their graves. It was more than just the few friends I'd been talking to. It was an entire village, a community all gone.

The demise of the old Blakeney was not sudden. Only slowly at first did its life ebb away, as its inhabitants were gradually replaced. The physical fabric of Blakeney remains but its soul has died. Some of the characters in my dream were themselves once newcomers, but they had arrived over a longer period of time and had become so well integrated over the years that they were quite indistinguishable from those born and bred here. The process of replacement began to speed up during the last three decades of the 20th century, and quickly the community I grew up in began to disintegrate. Looking back over my life, the most powerful recollections are from that earlier time. In so many ways they form the template against which I make judgments of the world as I experience it today. I firmly believe a meaningful sense of place is possible only if one's experience of it is four-dimensional - knowing not just how it is, but how it was.

There probably never was very much that local people could have done to protect themselves from what was to happen, although one far-sighted woman (herself an incomer) did. Blakeney was unbelievably lucky to have Nora Clogstoun. She not only had the vision to see what lay ahead for the indigenous population, but she also had the initiative to do something about it. She founded the Blakeney Neighbourhood Housing Society.

Walk down Blakeney High Street on a winter's night, and there are very few lights to be seen. But for the miracle of the BNHS there would be none. The entire heart of the village would be dark and lifeless. It is difficult to over-estimate how important the BNHS has been for local people. It is unlikely that there would be any indigenous inhabitants left if it had not existed. If you gathered together all the local people from the villages around Blakeney, as does happen from time to time (at Beano's funeral, for example), you would probably have enough to make one good village community.

But it's too late. As if enough damage hadn't already been done, politicians far removed from any sort of community have decreed, in the interests of equality, that any affordable housing built in north Norfolk (and quite a lot is being built) must be made available to any who might need it, no matter where in the country they come from. Of course if the whole country is your catchment, there will always be those with greater need than anyone local. At present there may be little we can do to hold onto the character of our beautiful towns and villages, and gems like Blakeney may in future be approached through homogenous affordable housing estates built on greenfield land to house people from the city. But if this place has taught me anything, it is that the future is always a surprise.

Weather forecasts, climate forecasts, economic forecasts seldom get it right, and the big stuff like the 1953 storm always comes out of the blue. I recall a series of lectures I attended given by a professor of what is currently called 'long wave' political and economic science, who had been involved at the very top and attended US /USSR summits. He was laying out a gloomy future for East-West relations when, halfway through, the Berlin Wall came down.

I live in Wiveton, a village which, like most in north Norfolk, has only a small percentage of indigenous people left, perhaps 10%, but it is a great community. It celebrated the Queen's Golden Jubilee with such style that it got itself on the front of two national newspapers. It did it again for the millennium, and it gave the parish council an idea.

Parish Councils have few powers and little opportunity to influence the shape of their village. But what we realised was that we did have the power to influence the shape of the community. We had just won an environment award and a £250 prize and when we were discussing what to do with it someone said, "Let's have a piss-up". Our very well trained clerk tried to squash the idea, so we rephrased it as Village Party. We had one, and we have had them every other year since.

Wiveton's population mix is eclectic, and I had concerns as to how it might work. There seemed a risk that it could fall out into social groups, so I spent most of the evening taking photographs and was delighted to discover that quite the opposite had happened. Everyone came together as villagers and neighbours.

This gave us the incentive to do more. A meeting was held between the parish council, the parochial church council and a village trust. The outcome was a 'Careline' system for the elderly and frail in the village. It is paid for by the village trust, administered by the PC, and those in need are identified by the PCC. There is no shortage of things to pull communities apart and these social gatherings apply an equal and opposite force that acts like a binding agent to pull it all back together. So I'll conclude with optimism - not a prediction but a hope that these ideas will take root and that while north Norfolk's villages may never again have the generational closeness they once had, they will nevertheless remain neighbourly communities where people care for each other. In the end, that is all that matters. People caring for each other is what makes a community and gives it life. So who knows? In another 50 years the villages along this coast may once again have a collective life similar to the one I knew as a child. That is my hope, forlorn perhaps, but it offers a future less bleak than it may once have seemed.

I am not a lone Cnut here, railing against the incoming tide, just the most recent. Nearly 40 years ago another Blakeney man voiced the same sentiments. These verses may not be John Betjeman, but despite that, or perhaps because of it, they paint a very evocative picture of the Blakeney that has been lost. I will let Ray Newland have the last word.

Blakeney Remembered
By
Ray Newland 1975

I dreamed a dream the other
night,
Saw Blakeney as it used to be,
Stood once again upon the hill
Through young eyes looking out
to sea
And in the foreground wide and
active
Ran the never silent quay
Children playing, sand and saltings,
Small boats sailing fast and free.

Wandered slowly up the High Street,
Paused a while to gaze in awe,
At a single stylish motor
Parked outside a rich man's door,
Passed the Anchor, pub not knitwear,
Smelt the tang of proper ale,
Heard from inside, muffled voices
Talk of cabbages and kale.

And opposite, the baker's shop
Mouthwatering smells I cannot call
One half penny's all I need
Alas I have no coins at all.
Up the street past myriad sweet shops
Alas I cannot help their trade.
On then to the British Legion
Bowls on perfect lawns are played.

To the cross roads, groups of people
Stand around and pass the day,
Safe enough to build a Maypole
For all the cars that pass that way
And to the Church, proud grey faced building
One certain thing they won't deface.

Nobly standing, dominating
Over years of human race.
Inside, lofty, cool, decorous,
Too young was I to note its treasures
Choirboy's robes, the Vicar's sermon
Keeping us from greater pleasures

And there were other things I did,
In summers where there was no rain,
Sitting horses, chasing rabbits,
Gathering the harvest in again,
Assisting older people
Draw their water from the well
Lusty youth, what happy memories,
Oil lamps with their musty smell.

Then came war, and with its end
Came water from the tap.
Electric lights and toilets new
Our place was really on the map.
To share its joys we once were pleased
With strangers from afar,
But with them came a host of things
Not least the motor car.

And piece by piece our heritage
Was steadily eroded
By endless modern garbage
With which those motorcars were loaded.
The trestle tables disappeared
From Blakeney's friendly pubs,
Replaced by gleaming ersatz bars
And made to look like clubs.

And now you see on summer nights
They all stand in a line
Each plastic man like the man next door
Sipping his glass of wine,
With open shirts and cravats
And yachting caps on heads,
As full of blooming character
As cabbages in beds.

We see again old Mrs Lubbock
Still dispensing pints of Two's
To leather booted country angels
Drinking ale, discussing news.
Not tales of far off cities
Nor news from distant hell,
But comfy, cosy, earthy topics
That they know and love so well.

Again we see bronzed Charlie Russell
Hitching up a team of four
He got them from the heavenly horse shop
Situated right next door.
And harvest in sunny August,
Is always good above the cloud
The difference is, they don't kill rabbits
That's definitely not allowed.

There are no storms to fright the sailor
The weather's good and the wind blows free
And sailing ships with produce laden
Again tie up at Blakeney Quay.

They've got a Garden Party
Where a boldly printed notice states
Jessie Burrows and her helpers
Are raising funds for heavenly gates.
Such minor lighting as required
Once more the oil lamp is the choice
And conversation, new, exciting
Using long forgotten voice.
And this time there is no mistaking,
They know where they went wrong before
And to that surge of plastic puppets
They'll firmly shut the door
From all, save one, they'll keep their village
Simple, happy, useful free,

All I hope, when I pass over, is
They'll find a little room for me.

34 Counting Cherries

Well, it happened. Just as I was putting this book to bed, we've had the biggest tidal surge for 60 years. In 1953 I was a child running the village streets with a wooden sword and dustbin lid shield. Now I am the Flood Warden for Wiveton. The results this time were very different: no loss of life and no structural damage to property, although there were plenty of flooded homes and businesses. Earlier in this book I made predictions for the chaos that I thought might ensue when the next surge came, they didn't come to pass, but only by the narrowest of magins. The sea defences put in by the Environment Agency over the years held up – just – and there was less flooding. EA dodged the crying-wolf bullet by putting out an unprecedented 48 hour warning, which I think woke everyone up, and to their credit they did see the big one coming.

The big difference between 1953 and 2013 was the wind. As I said in the earlier chapter, if you visualise all the elements necessary to produce a tidal surge as reels on a fruit machine, then you would need at least a dozen to come up cherries to generate the worst-case scenario. On Thursday 5th December, one very important cherry did not come up. In 1953 the centre of the depression tracked down the North Sea into Denmark and Northern Germany, dragging its fiercest winds down England's east coast. This time the depression moved away into Scandinavia, taking the strong winds with it, so as the evening wore on they began to drop, and at the crucial moment fell light.

This is my Flood Warden's account of that evening.

Although there have always been a few locals able to predict them, many tidal surge events in the past have come out of the blue. Today, satellite-based weather forecasts and digital media, coupled with local knowledge, offer opportunities to look a little further into the future. As early as 2nd December there was a clear indication that a very big tide was in the offing for the evening of Thursday the 5th. On Tuesday the 3rd this email went out to the Wiveton Flood Wardens:

John, Peter, and Steve, Thursday is a long way off but if the current timings for the arrival of the 'wind change' on Thursday remain in place there could be a very big tide and a possible breach of the Blakeney bank. Which of course is our cue to think about evacuations etc. I will keep you posted.

As the days went by and the wind-strength predictions increased, and crucially as the timing of the wind's change from SW to NW remained at five hours before high water, the likelihood of a major surge increased. For Blakeney, tidal flooding is a relatively gradual process, but for Wiveton, Cley and Glandford, all sitting behind the Glaven bank, a much faster-moving spectre lurks. Should the bank fail, then these three villages would go from dry streets to 20ft of water in as many minutes.

The first Glaven bank, erected shortly after the '53 storm, is a few feet lower than the new one that runs around the front of Cley Mill - something that would become significant as the night wore on. By late afternoon on the 5th, most of those in Wiveton who might need to be evacuated had been informed of the risk. The Flood Wardens came together at 6pm and, with torches and hand-held radios, went to look at the state of play at Blakeney. Pulling up over the rise, we were not surprised to see the Carnser deep under water, waves crashing against the Community Centre and the tide flowing over the road towards us – not good with another two hours to high water (and that was assuming the peak of the surge wouldn't come later).

We then went to check that the Environment Agency had shut the main sluice at Cley. They had, and we were able to go into the control room and see for ourselves the spinning gauge that showed how rapidly the water was rising. One of the EA team was standing in front of it as if hypnotised. Two of us went back to monitor the situation at Blakeney, where we could see water flowing over the bank like a weir. That it had come up so far in such a short time was alarming, so we quickly returned to see if anything had changed at Cley.

We stood by some Environment Agency steps – 12 of them, spanning a height of about 14ft – and decided that they would make a very good gauge of how quickly the water rose. We met the others where the old bank coming round from Blakeney joins the new one, and could see that the salt marshes were completely covered and a torrent of muddy water was starting to pour over the old bank into Blakeney Freshes. At this point they were still mostly dry, with just the ditches filling and giving off a powerful rotten-egg stench of sulphur, but then quite silently, as if welling up from the ground, a dark mass of water appeared, spreading fast. In seconds, all was covered by a fast-moving, foam-covered surface that in the light of our torches looked like a mighty river.

Hastening back to the steps we saw that four of them were already submerged. A fifth disappeared just minutes later. At this point I needed a pee and retreated to seek relief. By the time I returned (and without any help from me) another step had disappeared. By now the wind had died, the stars were bright and it was a lovely night. This calm gave the whole scene an eerie feel, like watching a train crash in slow motion.

As we swung our torches over the water we saw a hare swimming for its life. It was about 200 metres from safety, so we lit its way to the new shore. It took it a long time to get there but it made it. We then reflected for a while on the thousands of small lives that must have been extinguished while we were standing there. Within a very short time the water was three steps from the top and there were still 45 minutes to high water. We asked the Environment Agency men, who had retreated to their vehicle, if they could get us an update on the timing of the surge's peak.

They called their coordinators and came back with the rather frightening news that it was thought it had another hour to go. With the water still rising fast, they endorsed our decision to evacuate. Our evacuees, particularly those from bungalows, were taken to the Parish Room. Once we were certain that all were safe, we went back to the scene to find that the water had covered all the steps. It was within a foot of the top of the bank, and at a place where cattle had worn the surface down was slowly creeping over the top. If the wind had not eased there is no doubt that bank would have been overtopped – or, worse, it could have breached like the Blakeney bank. If that had happened, a 20ft wall of water would have rushed up the Glaven Valley and all the low-lying properties in Wiveton would have been inundated, bungalows submerged to the tops of their roofs and the main part of Cley flooded, with almost certain loss of life.

Aftermath

First thing next morning I went to Blakeney to record the damage and mark the height of the tide. On the north gable of the old coal barn at the bottom of the High Street are three plaques recording the flood levels for 1897, 1953 and 1978. My chalk mark sits at the top of a line of bricks that corresponds exactly with the mark for 1978. I then went to look at the damage elsewhere, and found the same bizarre redistribution of things as I had seen in 1953, when playing cards and cigarettes had been scattered around the quayside. This time I found a large clump of reedbed perched on top of a fence post, flights of steps leading nowhere, dead animals strung on barbed wire like a gamekeeper's gibbet and, where it wasn't breached, giant bites out of the sea bank. Some of these even looked to have teeth marks. It's almost as, if at the height of nature's assault on the works of man, a gate opens and the devil comes through to play in the chaos. There have been inevitable comparisons with the 1953 surge, and claims that this one was more severe – though mostly, I note, by people who were not alive in 1953. At Wells those claims may have some justification. In 1953 the west bank broke, allowing an enormous volume of water to spill into the reclaimed Holkham marshes.

This time the bank held. So it was a case of mixed blessings. The west end of the town stayed dry, but at the east end the flooding was worse. Having witnessed both events first hand, I can, without in any way diminishing the scale of 2013, tell you that for us there was no comparison. In 1953 there were hurricane-force winds, it was snowing and the wave damage was colossal. Boats were thrown through walls and houses were knocked down. On this occasion the failure of the Blakeney bank saved Morston just as the bank there was about to be overtopped and certainly reduced the flood level at Blakeney by about two feet, which somebody pointed out might have stopped it from reaching the level of 60 years ago. But of course the same bank also broke in '53. The significant difference was the wind. Sea defences are now very much better – EN have done a good job – but had the wind been blowing as hard as it did in 1953 I believe the damage and loss of life would have been just as great.

Afterthought

The flood defences put in over the years by EA did their job. They prevented many homes from serious flooding and undoubtedly saved lives, and they should be congratulated for that. But what is clear is that this was managed by only the narrowest of margins. Morston bank (rebuilt this year) would have breached if the Blakeney Bank hadn't broken, and both the Glaven and Stiffkey Valleys would have been inundated had the wind not eased. Between the lines of the descriptions above lies a device that could save serious flooding for many communities along this coast – "Pressure Release", for want of better words, meaning the deliberate release of water into reclaimed areas to take the pressure off property.

I was on the Client Steering Group for the most recent Shoreline Management Plan Review for our stretch of coast. The object of the plan was to put in place secure and sustainable defences against a projected sea level rise of one metre for the next century. It quickly became clear that very few of the current areas of "reclaimed salt marsh" could be sustained against such a rise,

and that realignment would eventually be inevitable. But such an idea would not be easy to sell, particularly to those directly affected, even if it meant that they would be better protected. It was argued that such controversial plans should be carefully explained to the public first. The new plan for Wells, was for new sea defences on a north-south line to protect the town's eastern flank. These would have the advantage of being sheltered from northerly fetch[1] and provide long-term security. A further advantage was that a lowered sacrificial section to the current (North Point) bank could have been installed, its height calculated to correspond with a flood level damaging to property. That section would then give way and take the pressure off the town. If this could been implemented it could have saved all the properties that were flooded in 2013. The idea was accepted by the EA and could have become a part of the plan if it had been properly explained to the public. It wasn't, and the public threw it out. These issues have far greater significance than saving a few hundred properties at Wells and Blakeney. Sea levels will continue to rise. What can be learned here can save lives and protect property everywhere.

1. Fetch = The distance available for wind to generate waves

**Further Acknowledgements
for
Images, Advice and Suppport**

Allen Frary
Graham & Diana Walker
Laurance Jordan
Peter Harvey
John & Geraldine Green
Carol Bean
Graham Lubbock
Mick Bensley
John Stevens
Mike Bennett
Bernard Bishop
Harry Bishop
Joe Reed
Roger Brett
Philip West
Richard Newton
The National Trust

Above are the names of those who contributed photos, drawings, maps and other information for this book, and to whom I am most grateful. I am also indebted to two others, Adrian Bell, sadly no longer with us but whose detailed vision of the countryside so chimes with my own, and Robert Macfarlane whose wonderful book 'The Wild Places' was the spur for me finally sitting down to write this book.

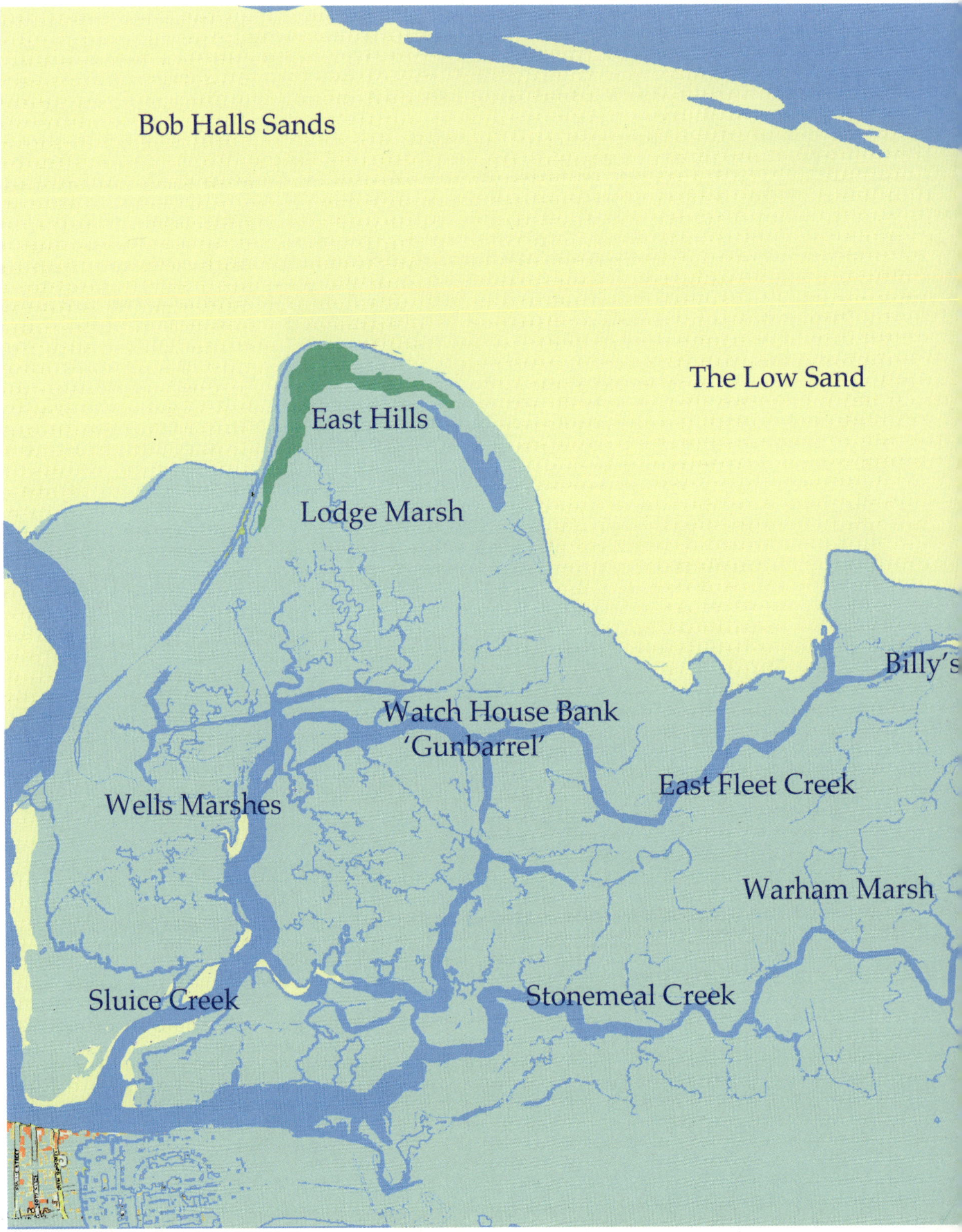

Bob Halls Sands
The Low Sand
East Hills
Lodge Marsh
Billy's
Watch House Bank
'Gunbarrel'
East Fleet Creek
Wells Marshes
Warham Marsh
Sluice Creek
Stonemeal Creek